The Faces of Death

Dianna Daniels Booher

BROADMAN PRESS
NASHVILLE, TENNESSEE

© Copyright 1980 • Broadman Press.
All rights reserved.

4254-24

ISBN: 0-8054-5424-1

Quotations from *The Living Bible, Paraphrased,* copyright © Tyndale House Publishers, Wheaton, Illinois, 1971, are used by permission.

Dewey Decimal Classification: 236.1
Subject headings: DEATH//CONSOLATION

Library of Congress Catalog Card Number: 79-53432
Printed in the United States of America

For Jeff and Lisa

Preface

Chances are if you're reading this book, you or a friend of yours has recently met death head-on. If that's the case, don't hesitate to first read the chapter which meets your need now. Then go back to the beginning to read the rest of the book.

Because we learn from each other, my plan has been to share others' experiences with grief to try to help you in your time of crisis. I'd like to thank those youth who have expressed so honestly their doubts, questions, hopes, and fears. Especially, I'm grateful to Debra Carpenter for sharing the story of her struggle with Hodgkin's disease (chapter 2). Also, I'd like to acknowledge the contributions of the researcher-pioneers in the area of death and dying. Their names are noted in the bibliography at the book's end. Finally, I'd like to thank Connie Thompson, librarian, who helped tremendously in gathering research materials.

If grief is yours, I hope you'll gain new insights to ease your pain. If you're reading this book to learn how best to help a friend, may God bless your efforts. Whichever the situation, you can teach others to live in the face of death.

Contents

1 Facing Death at a Distance 11
2 Facing Your Own Death 18
3 When Someone You Love Dies 36
4 When Someone You Love Is Dying 49
5 Helping a Friend Handle Grief 64
6 Psychological First Aid for Suicidal Friends 74
7 Is There **Really** Life After Death? 83
8 What Dying Says About Living 93
  Bibliography 95

> *To every thing there is a season, and a time to every purpose under the heaven: A time to be born, and a time to die.*
> *Ecclesiastes 3:1*

1
Facing Death at a Distance

"Can't we have a couple of pizzas for a snack before bed?" Bradley asked his mother as the family pulled into the driveway.

"I guess. If there's no horsing around. It's already late and tomorrow's school."

Bradley's basketball game was now a thing of the past. His parents and older brother Tommy had yelled their support, but Bradley had scored only ten points, a bad night for him. Silence had reigned on the trip home.

"Come on, Dad. Pizza's ready," Tommy yelled toward the hall twenty minutes later.

They heard the bathroom door open at the top of the stairs. Footsteps. Then a moan, a shuffle, a thud. All three pushed away from the kitchen table and ran into the hallway. Mr. Bagby lay at the bottom of the stairs clutching his chest.

A frenzied drive to the hospital. Stretcher. White uniforms. Waiting. Then the doctor reappeared in the emergency room lobby and motioned for Bradley, Tommy, and Mrs. Bagby. They searched his face and knew before he spoke.

"I'm sorry," the doctor said. "There was nothing we could do."

Even though you don't know the Bagbys, you probably feel shock, sadness, even anger when you read of their experience with death. Why? Death makes us uncomfortable. Even though it's "out there" somewhere, we try to hide from it. And when it sneaks up on us, we turn our face away and hurry in another direction. Ours, as some have termed it, is a "death-denying" culture.

We feel so deeply the need to avoid death that we often substitute other phrases for dying: passed away, made life's last journey, passed through the valley, gone to his final rest, gone to meet his Maker. We even try to lighten the subject with phrases like: kicked the bucket, croaked, cashed in the chips, gave up the ghost. No matter what the phrase, as long as it isn't "death" or "died."

But in this book, I want to talk about death plainly—when death is face to face, as well as at a distance. When asked to complete the statement "Death is . . . ," several youth responded this way:

- physically being gone.
- when the heart stops beating.
- when your body quits functioning and your soul leaves and goes to heaven or hell.
- when your brain and your heart stop working and your soul goes to heaven or hell—wherever it is supposed to go.
- the end of life as we know it.
- ending a life; the whole body stops working.
- physically, when the heart stops and will not supply blood to the organs and life ends.
- not living. However, if you don't have Christ, it is sort of like death now because you aren't really living.
- leaving your physical body behind.

Let me add three more technical definitions: clinical death occurs when the heart stops and breathing ceases. Biological

FACING DEATH AT A DISTANCE

death occurs when the tissues degenerate beyond function. Legal death occurs when the body does not respond to efforts of revival.

Most of these definitions sound cold because they describe death at a distance. But you cannot forever hold death at arm's length. It touches all sooner or later. When it does come close, you'll need to go beyond these definitions to cope with your feelings. I'd like to share some times I've come face to face with death and some thoughts and feelings with each meeting.

My first meeting—death and me—came in junior high school. The Curtis family and mine were close friends. We visited almost weekly and had even taken vacation trips together. Mr. Curtis was not feeling well and checked into the hospital for tests. Three days later after lunch at school, rumor spread down the hall; Mr. Curtis just died. His son, Eddie, was leaving school. My stomach knotted up. Not Mr. Curtis, "Edward" I called him. Who would take care of Eddie and his mother? He was my dad's age, too young to die.

Death came unexpectedly. To young fathers. It was scary.

In high school, I met death a second time.

Looking out the kitchen window, I saw Sue's car pull into the driveway. Behind her were Ida and Emily. Good, they were all on time. We needed the practice to get our cheerleading motions synchronized. Only two weeks until the first game of the season. I pushed out the back door and waited for them to get out of their cars.

Everyone was quiet, faces tense; something was wrong.

"We didn't know whether to come or not. Are we still going to practice?" Sue asked.

"What do you mean?"

"Didn't you hear about Larry?"

"No. What?"

"He . . . was in a wreck last night. He was . . . killed."

"Larry?"

"I thought you'd already heard."

"No. I didn't know. I can't believe it. Larry?" I kept repeating the words. I could still see his face and hear his voice as we'd talked in the school hallway the day before.

She went on to explain the details of the accident, but I heard few. What did you do when your girlfriend's sixteen-year-old brother had just died? Go to her house? The funeral home? At 9:00 in the morning? Someone mumbled that it was too early to go anywhere, that we should just practice for a while. My arms were heavy as I gestured and jumped. I mechanically mumbled the yells.

"I don't feel like it anymore."

"Me either. Me either. Let's quit."

And they were gone.

I sat down on the back step. Larry's voice sounded in my ears. I'd never gone out with him, but he'd asked me for a date several times. Now he was . . . dead. The idea was foreign. What was Carolyn going through now? What if it had been my own brother?

Later in the afternoon several girlfriends and I went to the funeral home. Silence most of the way. What could we say to Carolyn? To her parents? What were we supposed to say?

Inside the funeral parlor, Carolyn, with eyes red and swollen, sat alone on a couch near the coffin. As we entered, she came toward us. We all four embraced simultaneously; no one spoke.

Carolyn turned and led us toward the coffin. Then suddenly she leaned over on me with tears flowing again.

"I can't stand it," she cried. "I can't stand it. I loved him so much, but I didn't ever tell him. I can't stand it," she kept saying over and over.

I hugged her and let her cry in my arms. What to say?

Death happened to people my age—my friends, brothers.

The third meeting with death. Mr. Rollins came to the door of my college Bible study class and whispered, "Telephone."

Answering the telephone in the hall, I recognized my dad's voice,

"We've been trying to reach you all afternoon."

"I spent the afternoon at a friend's house. What's the matter?"

"Do you have someone there with you?"

"Yeah, why?" His tone sounded strange. "What's wrong?"

"Grandmother . . . died this afternoon."

"She did?"

Tears filled my eyes as I saw her face before me. It wasn't a surprise, yet it was. Six weeks earlier she'd fallen unconscious one morning and gone into the hospital for tests. She had inoperable cancer. Now, so quickly, she was gone.

I tried to get the details from my dad about where the family would be and the funeral arrangements, then hung up. Backing around the corner into an empty classroom, I sat down to take in the news. Grandmother's image flashed before me—a large, laughing woman, sitting in her rocking chair holding two of the smaller grandkids. I'd had plenty of turns in her lap, too. I remembered her playing with us. Shooting marbles. Jacks. Playing doctor (she was always the patient who got the shots). Playing beauty parlor (she was always the customer). Her laugh, her hug, her voice. All that gone. No more. Never. And I didn't even get to tell her I loved her one more time. Was she watching me now? Did she know how I felt? If I could just tell her I loved her one more time.

Death happened to our family. It hurt even more.

Since that time I've met death again and again. Sometimes at a distance, sometimes face to face. Each time, the pain of an earlier meeting comes to mind.

Yet, burying one's head in the sand when death occurs fosters the empty, purposeless lives so many people live. When you avoid death, deny its existence, you tend to have trouble with life. You go on preparing for tomorrow like it were sure to come. You never get around to living today to its fullest potential. You put off making a telephone call to someone. You don't bother to get "sentimental"—to say I love you or thank you. You neglect expressing what that certain friendship means to you.

To think about death does not mean to fear it. There's a difference. Fear is a learned response. Dr. David Gordon in his book, *Overcoming the Fear of Death,* points out that to struggle to live is instinctive in all animals and man. Yet, so far as scientists are able to tell, animals do not fear dying. Only man has learned this response from his culture.

Man fears death for many reasons. When the same group of youth were asked to complete the statement "What I fear most about death is . . . ," they responded this way:

- the suffering that might come before it.
- missing all my friends.
- that I don't know when it's coming.
- that I don't want to leave all my friends here. I'm scared of being alone.
- the uncertainty. I fear that I will tip the fragile scales that hold my life to my backbone.
- what it's going to be like.
- leaving the ones I love until they are sent to heaven too.
- the way other people would feel and the pain I might have.
- not being with family, friends. Not fulfilling your goals for life. But I know I will go to heaven so I'm not scared of dying itself.
- that I may never get to live my life completely.

One of the purposes of this book is to change these fears to awareness—that there is a definite cut-off point for accomplishments. Awareness that time will not go on forever makes us more alert to living each day to its fullest.

We'll consider death from several angles: Is it an enemy, a friend, or neither? Can science prove life after death? Where does God fit in? If he's in control, why do people die?

When death is face to face: How can I cope with daily life knowing someone in my family is going to die soon? How can I get over the hurt and pain when someone I love has died? How can I keep on going through the motions of living when I know *I'm* dying?

And when death is at a little more comfortable distance: How can I help when my friend is hurting over a death of someone he or she loved? How can I help my friend who has a serious illness and may be dying soon? How can I help a friend who is depressed and has hinted of killing himself?

Through what doctors, nurses, counselors, and others like yourself have to say about their own personal experience with death, I hope you can gain a new, clearer understanding of death as part of life.

To learn to die is to learn to live.

This world is the land of the dying; the next is the land of the living.
Tryon Edwards

2
Facing Your Own Death

Life has prepared us for many losses—losing a ballgame, losing an election, losing a pet. But how minor these losses when faced with losing your own life! It seems that no one is ever fully prepared to learn of a serious illness and the possibility of an early death.

I have not had to face such a shock. So I can't be an expert in telling you how to handle such an experience. I'm only a learner; I've read and listened to what seriously ill teens have thought, expressed, and hoped. In this chapter I want to share some of their insights and adjustments. In pulling you together with others in the same situation, I hope you'll be able to help each other. Then, in turn, you can teach us who have not yet faced such an experience.

Is it really possible to ever come to a point of acceptance about such a serious illness? Is it possible to ever be happy again? Debra, a twenty-year-old who has Hodgkin's disease, says so. Here is what she has to say about her experience of the last four years.

How did you feel when they first told you about the illness?

Well, it was a week before my sixteenth birthday. I'd just been going to a regular doctor. But he couldn't figure out what was wrong, so he sent me to a general surgeon. And then I went in to see the pathologist later. And when he was letting me get dressed, he told my dad to come into his office. He closed the door, and then he told my dad. So we get out to the car—me and my dad. He's wearing his sunglasses. In the building and everything. Hadn't taken them off. So I knew something was wrong. He was awful quiet.

I could see tears coming down his face. So I asked him, "What's wrong with me?" At first he didn't say anything. I guess he was just trying to figure out a way to tell me. When I had the surgery, they'd told my parents that everything was OK. But I imagine he—the doctor—meant the surgery was OK. No complications or anything. That's why my mother wasn't there. She said if she'd known it was something like this, she'd have come along. Then my dad said, "Well, . . . you have Hodgkin's disease." And I said, "What's that?" And he said, "That's cancer of the lymph glands." And the first question—I don't know why I asked him this—but I said, "Am I gonna die?" And (laugh) he didn't know.

It was just as foreign to him as it was to me. I didn't want anybody to know. I said, "OK, Dad. Don't tell Mother. Don't tell anybody." And he said, "That's ridiculous." I don't know. I just didn't want anybody to know. I guess I didn't want their pity. Usually when you think of cancer, you think of old people and you think of dying. You don't think of young people having it or being able to live through it. So it kinda threw me, you know. So when we got home, my dad took my mom into the bedroom and told her. She just came out and she didn't cry. I don't think I ever saw her cry about it. And I think that's one of the big things that kept me from being really depressed—seeing my parents hold up. That's the first time I'd ever seen my dad really cry.

Did you tell the kids at school?

No. I had just moved here and I was in a new school. I didn't know anybody to tell. Then that first tri-semester, I checked out. They had a homebound teacher to come around for kids who couldn't go to school. I believe I told an English teacher what I had. Because I found out through a friend of mine at church that she was a Christian. He knew because he had her for homeroom. So I felt like I could talk to her, you know?

How did your sisters take it? Did you tell them?
I don't remember. I imagine my parents told them. I know I didn't. And then everything just went about normal. I mean as normal as we could with me going to the hospital every day. It just surprises me how things go on as normal. It was like nothing was out of place. And that helped. You know, I hate when everybody just stands around and stares at you. And always asks how you feel. It's just like they expect you to pass out just any minute.

How long were you depressed when you first heard the diagnosis?
I don't really remember. About a week, I think. I just kinda sat around and went, "Wow. What's next?" But then I just tried to carry on like everybody else, and we got back to the same pattern.

What is your prognosis?
Well, if you've been in remission for five years, they say you're OK—you're cured. And I've been in remission for two years. Three more to go!" (Laughs.)

At any time, did you and the doctors or your family discuss the possibility of your death?
Yeah. When I went back in March after that first remission was over. The doctors took one look at me and said, "Well, we'll do what we can." But they weren't expecting me to make

FACING YOUR OWN DEATH

it either. But that's the only time they showed me any doubt—that I might die. They, I think, were really surprised that I made it. And now that I think about it, I am too! (Laughs.) I mean the way I felt and the way I looked. You know, those magazines that advertise children overseas who are starving and everything? Well, that's what I looked like. I could see myself in the mirror. I mean I could hardly get up out of bed without my knees giving away or something. And I couldn't keep my food down. They even had to push me around in a wheelchair.

Did your parents talk with you about death at that time?

No. I mean I knew I was close to it myself. But I never said anything about it. My parents never said anything to me. When I got real sick, they forbade my sisters to ever talk to me about it. For a while there, there were jokes about me being skinny. But then I kept getting skinnier and skinnier. And my folks said, "No, don't say anything more to her about it," you know. Of course, I didn't know about that then. I mean I didn't know anything until two weeks after I got out of the hospital and was on my way to fat city. That really surprised me. I mean like I didn't even know my dad had talked to Pastor Owen about having my funeral. I mean that really surprised me. I didn't even know I was that close! (Laughs.)

Would you have preferred that your parents had told you what was going on? How bad you were?

Yeah . . . . Yeah. I got on my mom about that. When it hit me that I could've died.

Do you still wish you could talk more openly about death?

Yeah. Especially about that—dying. Because I want to know what they think. As much as I want them to know what I think. I mean, I guess my parents would talk to me about it if I'd start a conversation with them. But they aren't going to start it with me, you know. Don't want to upset me. But I'm pretty sure I could talk to them.

What fears do you have now? That you'll come out of remission?

Yeah. That's the big one. I've heard that it'll come back. But I'm not so much afraid that I might die or about the treatments, but more along the line of having to go through all those tests again. I hate those tests. It's wait, wait, wait. And they just push you around like a piece of luggage or something. And they make you go without breakfast and everything.

How would you complete the statement, "What I fear most about death is . . ."?

Probably, . . . not knowing. OK, everybody has those doubts about whether they're going to go to heaven or not. That's not really a fear, though, for me. I think it's not knowing how it's going to be up there. You read in the Bible and you hear people giving their opinions and things. But you still wonder. That's going to be strange, you know. It's going to be different. (Laughs.) . . . Just not knowing. I know it's going to be great. But I guess it's just knowing that everybody else is still down here and that's where I'd really like to be. (Laughs.)

How about dating? Do you tell a boy that you're sick?

Yeah. Unless he already knows. The last few guys I dated already knew. The guy I'm dating now—he asks me questions about things he wants to know. Like I said, I don't mind talking about it.

How do they react when you tell them? Are they afraid to date you?

No . . . (laugh) not really until my dad gets hold of them.

What do you mean?

Well, we have this family joke. After I date a guy a few times, my dad'll pull him aside—where I can still hear—and he says, "Have you kissed her yet?" I mean what's a guy supposed to tell my dad? "No, Sir," or something? Especially after he has! Then my dad says, "You don't want to kiss her, you know. It'll make your tongue fall out." (Laughs.) I mean I thought I was gonna die the first time he said that to a boy.

Did anything unusual or embarrassing ever happen to you on a date?

Yeah. Once. When I was on the chemotherapy, my hair fell out and I had to wear a wig. Well, I was leaning over toward the dashboard, trying to find a good station on the radio. And this boy all of a sudden put his arm around my shoulder and started to pull me over to kiss him. And he caught the back of the wig and it came right off the back.

What did you do?

Nothing. I just grabbed it and pulled it back on, and I laughed. Then he laughed. And it was OK. But I sure was embarrassed. I was so glad it was dark and he couldn't see how red my face was!

How long did it take your hair to grow back?

Oh, about nine months. Yeah, on the chemotherapy it started to fall out and I started to wear the wig in March. But it grew right back—even while I was still on the treatments. I think it was in January that I took the wig off and had my hair cut and styled.

How about visitors? What did people say or do when they came to see you in the hospital or at home?

Well, there was this lady, a good friend of the family's. She was one of the finest ladies I've ever known. And she sent me a package—I got lots of nightgowns when I was sick—so it was a pretty nightgown. And in it was a card with this Scripture verse. Psalm 118:17. And it's, "I shall not die, but live, and declare the works of the Lord." And that's my favorite verse now. That's what I hold on to, I guess. She must have had the insight or discernment or whatever that the Lord was going to use me in a great way because of this illness.

How about friends your age? Did they visit you a lot?

Oh, yeah. I was always around the kids from church and everything. They were really good about coming to the house and the hospital, too . . . . Well, no one ever told me anything, but they would always come up to Dad and tell him how much—by watching me—they were strengthened, which made me feel good, you know. I was thinking, well, wow. I didn't think I was doing anything when they came to see me. But it was just being cheerful. I really tried to be that. But one thing I got irritated about was everybody always asking me, "How are you feeling?" I mean my mother just jumped all over me about that. I understand that they were concerned (laugh), but that question gets old. Everybody asked me that.

How else do your friends react when they are around you?

Everybody just goes about their normal way. This one girl, she's just plain crazy. Sometimes I wonder if she really has a brain. Well, about my scar. It's about this big (holds up fingers to indicate the length) and it's pretty wide. I'd always show it at slumber parties and stuff. My dad used to tell this girl that it was a zipper. And she believed it! Really, she believed him! And when we finally told her the truth, she said she believed it because they were coming up with so many new medical things that maybe they put in a zipper to get inside easier—some way they could open you back up without cutting. Can you believe that? And about the cobalt. My dad used to tell her and the kids who'd come over, "Hey, let's turn out the lights and let Debra glow in the dark." (Laughs.) Just like that, you know. That's the way it was handled. And the kids just picked it up from him. They saw me laugh about it and thought, if her dad does it, we can too. It was just all funny. Nothing cruel, I mean. Just funny. That's what got me through it all.

How about talking with your friends about more serious things—like your feelings about death?

Yeah, sure. I don't have anything to hide. I want to be open— talk about it. Tell them what it's all about. Yeah, I'd like for them to talk to me about it.

Did anybody ever cry when they came to see you? Or did you cry yourself?

No. Nobody ever did. Just me.

Did that embarrass you?

No . . . . No. One of my sisters is about as big a crybaby as me and she cried a few times.

Does it embarrass you to cry when you're talking about the illness?

No. But sometimes I just get choked up, you know. Sometimes I can talk about it all and never cry. I don't know what makes the difference. I guess it's just what mood I'm in or something. But usually when I cry it's by myself or with my parents.

How do you get over depression? And are there times you get really down?

There were, but not now. Since I'm not real sick now, I don't worry. How do I get over depression? . . . Music picks me up . . . having someone read to me. My mother has this soft voice. And when I was in the hospital and got so . . . you know . . . ho-hum, I'd like her to sit there and scratch my arm, and listen to her talk to me. Just be reassured of her love for me.

Are there things that changed in your life after the diagnosis? What became most important to you?

Probably, . . . my relationship to God. I mean there was a time I wasn't really strong. I mean I'm not saying I'm a superstrong Christian now, but my faith in him has increased. And my whole family, too. I want to keep my relationship more open than it was before I got sick. I'm making sure the communication lines are completely open and that I'm sure of what he wants me to do. You know, when you're in trouble like this, you make a lot of promises. "Just make me better and I'll be good." And I figure I probably got caught in doing that a lot. But other than that, I can't think of anything else . . . I just want to get to grow up, you know? I guess what I really want is to find someone to have a relationship with like my parents have.

Were you ever angry at God for allowing this to happen to you?

Yeah, I guess. You know, asking, "Why would God let this happen to me?" But I don't remember that much. Maybe some nights. Thinking, "Why me? What did I ever do to get this?" But not much.

Have you come to any answer about why—found any purpose in all this yet?

Yeah . . . You mean besides helping me to get closer to God? It helps others to be strong, too. Other people tell me

FACING YOUR OWN DEATH 27

and my dad how much it strengthens them to see how my family and I handle it. That's another reason. My dad even tries to get me to go down to the hospital and talk to kids my age and say, "Hey, look at me; I'm fine." To show that there's a chance they'll be OK, too.

What about hope? Have you always thought things would turn out all right?

Yeah, I always assumed it would. I never dwelt on the idea that I might not make it. I just always figured I would.

You don't fear death now at all? Don't ever think about not making it?

No. It doesn't enter my mind. I'm OK now; I guess that's why. But if I die, I die, you know? If it's my time, then I know I have a place up in heaven waiting for me. I'm happy now. I have a good job. I'm dating this guy I like very much. I just got a new car.

How about marriage plans for the future?

Well, that's definitely on my mind. That's what I'm looking forward to someday. Having kids and a happy marriage.

What would you advise others to do to adjust to something like this?

To keep their mind off it, mainly. Just go about your daily routine as much as possible. I know it's hard with the treatments and all. But just depend on the Lord. I mean, he's the only thing. The only one who got me through it. My mother—when she went with me to the doctor and sat in the waiting room while I was having the tests—she talked to some other people waiting for the doctor. And you know, lots of those people down there just don't have anything to grasp hold of. They don't have any beliefs or anything. Mother said she didn't think she could've made it, you know? And I feel the same way. I mean, he's the thing."

Debra's feelings may not be yours right now. She has had time to absorb the shock and work through her emotions. If you've just recently learned of your illness, you may want to go back and consider at a slower pace some of the things Debra mentioned. Let's do that now:

Hearing such words like Hodgkin's disease or leukemia is scary. But despite the fear, most teens say they are glad to know the truth about their condition. It's like a game of pretend when you're denied the truth. You can't share your inner thoughts and fears with your family or friends and help each other with the grief.

If you ask, most doctors and parents will tell you about the seriousness of your illness. Your asking is their indication that you really want to know and can accept the pain that comes with the news. Feel free to ask all the questions you have in mind. Fear of the unknown can be much worse than reality. Asking questions can help you understand better how to cope with your sickness and treatment.

But no doctor can ever tell you with certainty that you will die. He can tell you that some patients who have your disease live approximately a certain number of years. But there are always people who live much longer. And virtually every doctor in the country can tell you of patients cured and restored to health beyond all explanation.

New treatments and drugs are discovered almost every day. Just think of all the diseases that were killers only a relatively short time ago—smallpox, tuberculosis, polio. Huge sums of money are invested every year in research for cures. Dr. Jan van Eys, the head of the Pediatrics Department of the University of Texas System Cancer Center, says there is an "almost infinite" distinction between false hope and real hope. In other words, even though he works with cancer patients every day, he, and many other doctors agree, says there are virtually no hopeless cases.

No one but God knows the time of your death.

One of your primary concerns if you have a serious illness, then, is to maintain your hope and not give up. You noted that ingredient in Debra's story! All doctors agree that your attitude affects your physical fight against disease. Hope is real. Don't give up.

But alongside hope, fear will sometimes creep in. And often this fear is not fear of actual death, but things involved in the *process* of dying. One such fear is of being a burden to others. You may feel like a burden when brothers and sisters have to rearrange their plans to accommodate your needs. You may fear the trouble you are causing your parents—their trips to the hospital and the expense. If this is one of your fears, turn the situation around and think about the illness as if it were another family member's. Would you mind going to the hospital to see him or her? Would you mind spending your money if you thought it would help? Neither do they. It's called love.

Another fear is that of terrible pain. It's easy to have this fear because so many movies show painful, violent deaths. But doctors assure us that most pain can be controlled by pain-killing drugs.

A third fear is that of losing physical good looks and abilities. This, too, is an understandable fear because some drugs do have side-effects which cause swelling, weight loss or gain, skin sores, or other things. If you have this fear, it may help to reverse the situation again. You probably do not base your friendships and love on someone's physical appearance. Neither do other people. And as in Debra's case, altered physical appearance can be only temporary.

Another fear most youth have is losing relationships. You love parents, brothers, sisters, and friends deeply. It is painful to think about having to give up those relationships. One way to help alleviate that fear is to spend as much time as possible now with these people. Time together is not always measured in quantity of years together—but in quality of the relationship.

Another fear is facing the unknown. Despite all the present-day research, we know little about death. People are afraid of most anything they have no knowledge about. Fear of the unknown is much like taking a history exam. The prospect is much more frightening when the teacher has told you nothing about it than if she's given you a list of sample questions. Or, consider your feelings when walking into a strange house in the dark. It would be much easier to follow along behind someone who knows the way. It may help you to realize that if you are a Christian, Jesus is leading the way and will have the light on just inside the next room.

All these fears—pain, being a burden, altered physical appearance, losing important relationships, the unknown—are understandable. Others have had these same fears; you are not alone.

Because many or some of these fears come rushing at you when you learn of your illness, you may want to deny that you are even sick. You may feel that if you don't talk about it, it will all go away. Some teens have even gone so far as to refuse to take medicine or to follow doctor's orders, trying to prove to themselves and others that they're not really sick. Denying that you're sick is a protection from emotional pain. We all deny things are really happening at various times in our lives.

Another feeling you may have is intense anger—at your family, at friends, at God. Adolescence calls for emotionally pushing away from your parents—developing your own friends, interests, and future. A serious illness traps you in the middle of the breakaway. You need your family for emotional support with the illness and you also need to stand on your own. All that emotional struggle back and forth can lead to hostility toward your parents. Feeling like a burden to your parents, too, can make you feel guilty. That guilt, then, makes you even angrier.

You may also feel angry at your friends. If your friends continue to come around like Debra's did, you can appreciate their maturity to handle their own fears about death. But if your friends fail to come around, it can be a devastating blow. Immature teens may feel uncomfortable around someone who is very sick because they don't know what to say. They don't want to say something to make you feel worse. They may be afraid that if they tell you all about the things going on at school, it will make you want to be there even more. On the other hand, if they don't talk about school and their activities, they don't know what else to say. So, they may just fail to come around. Understanding the "whys" may lessen your anger.

Sometimes you may even be angry at God. Why me? you may wonder. You feel cheated and frustrated that you are so young to be so sick. Parents and teachers are always urging you, "Take this harder course to get ready for college," Or, "Save your money for a car." Then when you find out there may not be a future for you, you feel cheated and lied to.

Why you? It's not easy to know why God permits something to happen to you, or why he doesn't work a miracle to heal you. Some illnesses and accidents come just because God gives man a free will and lets him run his own life. Sometimes people do careless things which bring harm to themselves or to others—such as air pollution. Sometimes freak accidents of nature happen. God has set up laws of nature, like gravity, for common good. For God to keep intervening with these laws would make the world a chaotic place to live. Sometimes God permits illnesses "for his glory." He may want to perform a miraculous cure to bring people's attention to his purposes and plan. Sometimes God permits illness to show people how dependable he can be. He wants people to trust and depend on him instead of being proud and independent.

And sometimes God permits things to happen for reasons unknown to men. No matter how much you try to figure it out, you can't. If not understanding a reason or purpose makes you angry, talk out your anger to God. That's what King David did. (Read Psalm 22:1-20 from *The Living Bible, Paraphrased*). God is a big powerful God who loves you despite anger or doubts. Express your pain and hurt to him as others have done; he can give you understanding.

After feelings of denial and anger, you may gain new hope, as Debra mentioned, by bargaining with God. You may promise that if he'll just let you get well, you'll devote the rest of your life to some worthy cause. And God has been known to heal people miraculously—maybe for just such reasons. King Hezekiah asked God for more time and was granted fifteen more years of life (2 Kings 20:1-6).

But if such is not God's will for you, you may fall into a deep depression. When you think about facing more new drugs or treatments, you may feel as though you don't much care anymore. You may want just to be alone during this time. You may feel physically weak and need more rest. At times, your hope for recovery may all but fade.

At other times, you will overcome this depression and be able to look at your illness with acceptance. Acceptance is saying, "OK, these are the facts. This is most probably what's ahead." On that assumption, you begin to rearrange your life and priorities.

Acceptance is realizing that there are things much worse than dying. One person with a terminal illness, quoted Martin

Shepard in *Someone You Love Is Dying*, spoke about her approaching death this way:

"It [death] is not the worst thing in the world that can happen to you. Really and truly. I feel I would rather have this than be blind. I would rather have this than have no arms. Everything is relative to the individual. In your own mind you decide, 'What is the worst thing in the world that could happen?' And I don't think that dying is it."

I remember the first time I confronted the idea that death was relative. My dad phoned me at college to say that my grandfather had been in a car accident. "How bad is he?" I asked. My dad proceeded to tell me the details of his many injuries. But all that kept running through my mind as I listened was, "Is he going to live?" Anything, but death. I just wanted my dad to tell me that Granddaddy would not die.

"But I mean, he isn't going to . . . he'll be all right, won't he?" I asked again.

"I don't know, Dianna, . . . but there are a lot worse things that could happen to him than death."

I have never forgotten that idea. Very few people can see life and death so clearly.

You possibly have not experienced all these feelings—anger, bargaining, depression, and acceptance. You may never. On the other hand, these are common feelings of many seriously-ill youth. Understanding why you have these feelings may help you work through them or toward them.

However, the most important thing you can do when you are facing a critical illness is to make spiritual preparation. If you have any doubts at all about what will happen to you after death, read chapter 7. Don't delay in asking God to come into your life. Whether you have one year or one hunded years of living ahead, you'll never be sorry for that decision.

During such a crisis time as illness, only very mature people can think of others. If you are one of these persons, here are some ways you can help others even in the face of your own death.

First, you may want to make provisions for donating parts of your body to someone else. Such love for someone you don't even know is one of the highest forms of Christian giving. Talk with your parents about it. If there is an office of The Living Bank in your area, ask them for information.

Another way to help others at this time is to ease any unreasonable guilt your family has. Parents, especially, are often filled with regrets. You can express to your parents that you don't blame them for your illness and that you know they are doing all that is possible to make you well and comfortable. Parents will remember your concern for their feelings forever.

A third way you can help others is to be a model and a teacher. One way to help those of us who have not faced your situation is by writing down your thoughts—good and bad. Many people have kept such a record—a diary or journal either daily or spasmodically. Those treading the same waters for the first time have gained courage through reading of another's struggles, insights, and methods of coping.

Another way to be a teacher is through your attitude about your situation. It may be a goal of yours to make those around you feel at ease about death. You can be a model of how someone faces such a crisis with hope and faith. Your attitude can be a lifetime inspiration for your family and friends.

Another way to teach is to share your faith in God. One sixteen-year-old shared her faith in God's goodness by planning her own funeral as a testimony and encouragement to others to get to know her God. As a result of her funeral, four persons came to talk to the minister about how they might come to know God in such a meaningful, trusting way.

A pastor friend of mine explains that in a sense those who know about soon-approaching death are lucky. Although an odd way to express this thought, he goes on to explain that most people tend to live as if life would go on forever. They waste day after day in trivial pastimes, in regretful words and actions. When you know death is approaching soon, you tend to rearrange your priorities—to savor every moment.

Make your remaining time—whether a month or many years—meaningful. Teach us to do the same.

We understand death for the first time when he puts his hand upon one whom we love.
Madam de Stael

3
When Someone You Love Dies

The pain of losing someone you love through death is called grief. Grieving is a time of painfully adjusting to a new loss and a new situation. It's a time of struggling to remain a whole person in control of mind, emotions, and body.

If you've experienced a death of someone close to you, then you know some of the feelings involved in readjusting to life. When you're hurting, sometimes it helps to know that others have passed through this same pain and recovered a stronger person. Their strength fosters your courage. Also, knowing what may still be ahead for you can help you prepare for other grief-related problems. So the purpose of this chapter is to help you understand and work through your grief pain and problems.

The word *grief* covers several reactions over an indefinite period of time. Grief pain is both mental and physical. Physical reactions may include: a tightness or lump in your throat, difficulty in breathing, a choking feeling, frequent sighing, weakness in your muscles or involuntary contractions, weakness and tiredness even after sleep, chills, tremors, tenseness, slowness in doing ordinarily quick jobs, stomach feels hollow and empty, food is tasteless, objects may appear to be farther away and harder to see, or hallucinations about seeing the dead one.

You may experience a few, some, or all of these feelings

after the death of someone you loved. You are already aware of how the mind and body are connected by emotional stress in such illness as ulcers, heart attacks, high blood pressure, and headaches. So it is with grief pain. Your body reacts to the stress in the above ways. All of these are normal reactions and will pass as you work through the grief and readjustment period.

We humans are made so much alike that we even experience similar mental pain. Many kids sometimes feel that they are losing their mind—that everything inside will explode under the pain. You may be feeling the same stress and wondering how others have coped. Dr. Elisabeth Kubler-Ross has investigated some "stages" you may go through in adjusting to such a great loss.

The first stage is shock or denial. When learning of a sudden accident, you make statements like: "It can't be true." "I just saw him." "I don't believe it." "She was too young to die." "You're mistaken." Your mind stalls for time to comprehend the fact of death. You totter between reality and fantasy. One minute, you feel the pain of the idea that the person is gone forever and all the implications that involves. The next minute, you have no feeling at all. Everything seems like a dream from which you will awake to find it all untrue. Even physical numbness sets in during this stage of shock or denial.

The funeral service plays a big part in helping you overcome this shock and move on in working through the pain. Going to a funeral home, seeing the body, hearing a memorial service is extremely beneficial in helping you face reality. Hearing people express their sympathy forces you to realize and focus on your loss. Although painful to face the reality, the funeral experience speeds up the end of your pain.

The second stage of grief is usually anger—anger caused by fear or guilt. If your parent has died, you may fear the future. You wonder about practical things like money matters and who will provide for you. You may be particularly fearful if you hear the remaining parent say something like: "I don't want to go on living without him (or her)." Or, "There's not enough money; we can't make it alone." Such statements are common when people are under stress, but they won't mean them later. Still, the thought of being abandoned without anyone to care for you is frightening.

This fear often turns into anger. You may become angry at God and question why he would let something like this happen to you. You may turn that anger against the person who died. You may be angry that your dead parent "deserted" you. You may be angry at him or her for not getting a check-up sooner or being more careful, if the death was an accident. You may turn that anger toward a hospital staff or other family members or friends. You may think that if only the doctor had gotten to the hospital sooner, or the nurse had checked the records more carefully, the death wouldn't have occurred. You may be angry at a family member because he or she wasn't home to prevent the accident. You may become angry at outsiders simply because they are still living, and they are not hurting like you are.

Of course, consciously, you don't think through the reasons behind your anger to see that they are illogical. Feelings are irrational. On the surface, all you know and feel is anger, hurt, bitterness.

Another cause of anger may be guilt feelings. Almost every professional who deals with grieving persons recalls that most people feel some sort of guilt. Some people feel guilty because they think they should have been able to prevent the death or that they somehow caused it. A son may feel that his bad grades caused his father to die of a bleeding ulcer. In reality, his father's stress may have been due to his job situation.

Another reason one may feel guilty is past actions or words against the one who has died. Karen had always teased her little brother about being an "egghead" and reading instead of playing outside with the neighborhood boys. When her younger brother was killed accidentally, all she could think about were her taunting words to him.

Sometimes people may feel guilty about past thoughts or actions against their loved one. Melanie secretly thought her mother always dressed sloppily and neglected her hair. Although she never expressed these feelings aloud, after her mother's death, she felt guilty about being ashamed of her mother's appearance.

Another reason for guilt is feeling relief at the death. Mackal's father, an alcoholic who was dying of cirrhosis of the liver, had been hospitalized numerous times. All the family's money had gone to pay hospital bills. His mother was worn out going between the hospital, her job, and home to care for the smaller kids. Even though Mackal loved his father, after his death, he had a sense of relief that the long ordeal was over. Yet, he felt guilty about the relief.

Guilt for any of these reasons, like the fear I mentioned earlier, usually turns into anger. You may feel angry toward someone else, the one who died, or yourself. If you can understand that some of your anger is caused by guilt—either deserved or undeserved—you can work through it.

Many counselors suggest paying off the "emotional debt" by talking with someone about your guilt feelings. Praising the dead one's good qualities to another person makes you feel as though you are "making it up" to the one who has died. Also, by admitting bad feelings and attitudes, you can receive someone else's forgiveness. After someone else understands and forgives, you can forgive yourself more easily.

Fixing the blame for the death on someone—either yourself or others—only prolongs getting on with the readjustment you have to make. Talking out those feelings of guilt, fear, and anger help them pass.

After denial and anger comes the third period of intense grief—depression. This particular depression period takes over when you have finally accepted the reality of death and raged against yourself, God, and others. You then settle down to face the consequences of life without that person.

Tears come easily. You can't eat or sleep. You may find yourself sitting and staring at the floor or the walls. You don't feel like talking to anyone. You don't want to enjoy any of your favorite activities. Immense feelings of loss, helplessness, and hopelessness come flooding over you.

After this period of intense depression comes the final period of adjustment—acceptance. After working through all the other feelings, you decide that you will not die, that you must go on living. You have not forgotten the loved one at all, but you have accepted the reality of death. You now accept the challenge to move on with life in spite of the loss.

Of course, not everyone will pass through each of these phases, but they are common, normal reactions. You can receive help and comfort in knowing that others have experienced these same emotions and have reached adjustment.

But remember that grief is an individual process. After the death of someone you love, you may not pass through one or any of these stages before acceptance. Leon displayed no outward emotion when his grandmother died. For months she had suffered with cancer. He, as well as most of his family, had already passed through these stages—denial, anger, depression—before his grandmother's death. They mourned and grieved each day as she grew worse. At her death, Leon had no feelings of anger or depression left, only acceptance of the fact that he had already lost his grandmother when she became ill. This process is called "anticipatory grief," grief that occurs when you know about a loss before it actually happens. It, too, is a normal reaction.

Because grief is an individual matter, all the family members must be tolerant and understanding of how each expresses his or her own grief. Some people may be vocal about grief; others may be silent. Some may find relief in humor, which others find disturbing. One sociologist, Martha Wolfenstein, has done a study on humor at the time of death. She found that many people tell jokes or laugh about something funny the dead person did to relieve tension and pain. They do not mean such lightheartedness as disrespect. It is only their way of getting some relief from pain.

Another person may express his grief by spending hours with the body of the loved one before the funeral. Another person may feel the need to get far away. Scott, when his best friend died, felt relief in getting outside, walking, and driving around to the places where he and his friend had spent time together. His dead friend's parents couldn't understand why Scott didn't spend more time with them at the funeral home. They didn't understand that he was showing his grief in another way, more meaningful to him. If someone seems to resent what you're doing, you may have to explain why you are reacting in a certain way. Explaining your feelings to one who questions your behavior may help both of you cope. During a time of grief, everyone is under intense pressure. Try to be tolerant of others' expressions of grief.

As you pass through these emotional stages and move toward adjustment, other problems may arise—problems with friends' reactions, with memories of the loved one, with readjusting to daily schedules and activities. Let's consider these.

During the grief process, you may have unreasonable feelings toward your friends, and they to you. You and your friends may have avoided each other and withdrawn emotionally. Friends may fail to come around you because they don't know what to say and don't want to cause you to cry. Tears are a great release and good for you, but unfortunately, friends may not know that. And when they do come around, they may not know that you really want to talk about the death. Instead they may talk about the weather, the football game, the food.

In such a case, you will have to educate them about how to treat you. If you broke your leg at the top of a mountain climb and had to be carried down, certainly you'd tell your friends how to lift and maneuver you to lessen the pain. So it is with the pain of grief. You may have to tell them outright you'd like to talk about something your father always did or said. And even after the initial time of grief, your friends may still be hesitant about talking about their own families for fear of making you think of your loss. You can put them at ease by bringing up the subject and asking about their family. They will gradually feel more comfortable around you, and you can resume your normal relationship.

Other people may avoid mentionng your loss because of fear. Your grief reminds them of what could happen to themselves. Understanding their fear can help you avoid anger at their silence.

On the other hand, your friends' withdrawal may be due to your own anger or bitterness. One girl writing about her father's death in *event* magazine says, "I went back to school a week later. I tried to apologize and make up with the friends I had shunned, yelled at, ignored, and even hated for five months. I had blamed them for deserting me when I needed them most. In reality it had been I who had withdrawn from them. When we were together during those months of my father's illness, I had heaped on them all my anger and fear."

You, too, may feel this same resentment. But understanding why friends don't talk about the death may help you forgive their failures rather than become bitter and push them further away.

Another problem when someone you love has died is the fear to love someone else. But even though you fear loving and losing someone again, another loss would be far better than never loving again. Loving others and having them love you is vital to your mental health.

Another problem—the opposite of the fear to love again—is becoming overly involved emotionally with a substitute for the person you lost. Because at the time of a loss you feel weak, isolated, and alone, you may reach out to someone else who shows concern in an unusual way. Susanne's mother died when she was thirteen after a long bout with cancer. Her piano teacher, Miss Haverty, had shown special concern and went out of her way to take Susanne under her wing. She had visited the hospital a few times during the mother's illness and frequently asked about how things were going at home. When Susanne's mother died, Susanne fantasized abut how nice it would be to have Miss Haverty for a stepmother. In subtle ways, she began to hint to both her teacher and her father that she wished they could get together. When she learned that neither one had an inclination to begin such a relationship, Susanne was crushed. She had "overinvested" emotionally in someone at a time when she was lonely. Don't be afraid to accept emotional support and caring from others during your grief; you need support. But try to maintain your balance and not let your emotions run away with you in trying to replace someone you've lost through death.

Memories can be another area of confusion. Ida LeShan, writing in *Learning to Say Good-By,* describes two different kinds of memories. The first are memories of images and physical qualities of the person—the smell of tobacco, handshakes or hugs, laughter. Gradually the memories of physical things fade into memories of feelings—special vacations, playing tennis together, teasing about your boyfriend/girlfriend relationship. These memories are your way of holding on to that person forever. You can never lose what that person meant to you as long as you have those memories.

Some people have gained satisfaction by writing down these memories in a special diary or journal and collecting pictures of that person as a memorial to refer to again and again in later years.

Of course, this type of memorializing can be taken to an unhealthy extreme. Todd and his father shut off the mother's room as soon as she died. For years they kept the room just as she had left it—the same bedspread folded back across the foot of the bed, her clothes in the closet, her make-up out on the dresser. This type reaction is unhealthy and keeps the grief wound bleeding.

Others may feel that memories bring too much pain; they want to forget immediately. They may give away all the dead person's belongings. But it is best to wait before deciding what to give away and what to keep. When the pain subsides after a few weeks, you can decide more clearly. You may try to forget by refusing to do things or go places which you enjoyed together. Though forcing yourself to reexperience these activities and places is difficult, it has a healing effect.

Holidays often bring especially painful memories. Rearranging rituals and schedules helps. Instead of spending July 4 on the beach, go to the mountains. Instead of opening your birthday presents at dinner, open them at breakfast. Any such variation helps you enjoy the occasion as a new event rather than compare it to past ones.

Another problem with memory is that it's inaccurate. You tend to idolize a loved one who has died. You have seen this idolization at work in news of current events. When a national leader or entertainer dies, all kinds of statements and books about how good he or she was come out. People tend to forget the mistakes the person was criticized for while living. Such praise is intended to honor and express love. The intention is good. But the greatest respect is to remember the dead just as he or she was. To remake someone's character in your memory doesn't necessarily show love for what he was in reality.

And such inaccurate memories can even be harmful. You may make extreme statements of praise out of a sense of guilt for something you said, did, or thought while that person was living. This guilt needs to be dealt with by talking it over with someone else rather than covering it up with praising statements.

Another reason inaccurate memory can be harmful is that your loss seems much greater. When you forget about all the bad arguments your parent and you had, forget that you yelled at each other frequently, forget that he or she wasn't perfect, you feel even more empty for having lost something so valuable.

Another thing about inaccurate memory is that it leads to unfair comparisons. You may find yourself thinking, "Dad would have let me do that; Mother treats me too babyish." Or you may even say to your other parent, "Mother would have given me a bigger allowance; she wasn't selfish like you are." In intense anger, you say things which hurt the other parent deeply. Such feelings are cause for checking up on the accuracy of your memories. Realize that you have forgotten some of the normal, not-so-good qualities of the person who has died.

Another problem that comes up when you have lost someone you loved is whether to tell others about your loss. Bryan was accompanist for the school choir. The director had planned a special shopping mall concert on April 19—the night one year earlier when Bryan's younger brother had died. Bryan had wanted to spend the night alone at home with his parents. But other choir members had been complaining about the concert because they didn't want to tie up a Friday night. Bryan didn't know if he should tell the choir director why he didn't want to come to the program on that particular night. He was afraid the director and the other kids would think he was just using his brother's death as an excuse.

In such situations you have to be the judge about whether to tell others. If you need special consideration or if you think it is only fair and thoughtful to let another person know why you're acting in a strange way, tell. But if your motive is to gain unfair advantage, to get out of something, to manipulate someone or something, don't. Be honest.

One final consideration in working through your grief is that you must take positive steps to readjust. At first you may have to make yourself go on with living—to go to a movie, to spend the weekend at a friend's house, to bake a batch of your dad's favorite cookies. You may not enjoy the time at all. In fact, you may cry through it. But each time you force yourself to function in a normal way, the next time will be easier. One, two, then three steps slowly and you gradually will find yourself walking life's road again.

It may be a long time after you're again a functioning individual before you realize any good from the pain of loss and problems of readjustment. Yet, many kids talk and write about personal growth through such experiences. Let me share some of the insights and good others have expressed as a result of great sorrow.

Many have learned to value each day of life. They've learned to say "I love you" with no tinge of embarrassment. They learned to spend time together as a family. They learned to say encouraging things to others when they were down. Guilt from past neglect has caused them to mend past mistakes and enrich their future.

Others have learned compassion. When they've felt the ache inside themselves to talk to others about their loss, they've learned to give others a chance to talk about their own hurt. Nothing brings people closer together than sharing grief sorrow.

Others have turned their grief into good by devoting time

or money to special projects. Parents who've lost a child to leukemia have devoted efforts to raising more money for research. Hospitals and orphanages have been built out of people's desire to memorialize a loved one. If you've lost a younger brother or sister to a fatal disease, you may want to devote time to entertaining sick kids in the children's ward of the hospital or in tutoring a neighborhood kid who's having trouble in school. You'll find that through such effort toward another person or project, your own pain decreases.

For others, grief has brought spiritual growth. Many kids find out at the time of death that they have had a secondhand faith. When death intrudes, they have to sort out what they personally believe about God and afterlife. David Book, in *event* magazine, writes that his faith was strengthened through the death of his best friend. At first he blamed God for the friend's car accident. Gradually, he came to realize that God had not caused the accident, that he gave man free will to choose and to take risks. His best friend and he had taken a risk and driven too fast on a wet road. That was not God's fault. David's experience in reaffirming God's goodness is similar to that of many who have suffered such a loss.

Finally, there's the confidence and peace that you have just passed through life's ultimate test—death. Do you remember how it feels to get through the one semester exam you dread the most? After the *big* one, the others are inconsequential. The thought that nothing can be more startling or painful than death can be comforting in facing an uncertain future. You have come through life's worst.

To learn to live each day to its fullest, to help others by showing compassion, to work for good causes, to reexamine and strengthen your faith, to gain peace and confidence—all these can stem from the death experience.

Grief is an expression of love. Just as I wish I could have told my grandparents one more time how much I loved them,

I have been comforted by the thought that they watched my grief from heaven and knew.

But life, too, is an expression of love. To want to go on with living and to recapture through new relationships the happiness you've shared with the dead one is a great compliment. To share love is to risk grief. But life is worth the risk.

In time, the joy of having loved will overshadow the pain of grief.

> *Each departed friend is a magnet that attracts us to the next world.*
> *Jean Paul Richter*

4
When Someone You Love Is Dying

Sheryl overheard her mother's phone conversation with the doctor. "What's the matter?"

"Oh, they want to do some more tests. Take a tissue sample and check it. I think they just see how many tests they can do to get a little more insurance money."

Her mother's face relaxed; Sheryl was relieved. Everything was OK, nothing serious.

Two afternoons later when Sheryl came home from school, her dad and mother were home. When she walked in the door, she knew something was wrong. Her mother's red and puffy eyes and her dad's tensed expression disturbed her. When she persisted in knowing what was the matter, her dad pulled out a chair for her from the kitchen table and told her to sit down.

"Your mother has a malignancy—cancer."

To know in advance that time will soon stop for someone you love—whether friend or family member—is the severest shock you'll probably experience short of the actual death experience. When Sheryl heard the news, she wanted to cover her ears and run from the room. But at the same time, she did want to know the truth. She didn't want to be an outsider, unable to share the family's grief when they needed her the most.

Whether to tell the patient and all the family about a serious illness is a difficult decision for both the doctor and family. Such a decision will necessarily involve you because you'll have to conduct yourself accordingly.

At first, to pretend sounds easier or less painful, but you can understand how such pretense would eliminate meaningful discussion of your feelings. That's why counselors emphasize how important it is that a patient know when he is seriously ill.

You may need to encourage your family to be honest and open in their death situation. This lets you be supportive of each other through such a painful time.

This same policy applies to younger children in your family. Even though you won't be responsible for making the final decision to tell them that one of your parents or another family member is seriously ill, you can encourage your parent to be honest with them. Professionals agree that if a younger brother or sister is old enough to ask questions, he is old enough to get answers.

But if your brother or sister feels especially close to you, you may be the one they ask questions of and express feelings to. If you are unsure about how to answer, take them to your parents and help them ask their question.

If for some reason that is impossible, you will need to know how to respond to his or her questions yourself. Try to answer honestly, but don't over-answer. To make sure how much your brother or sister wants to know, Dr. Easson, in his book, *The Dying Child*, suggests asking questions like, "What do you mean? Exactly what are you asking?" Kids under nine or ten years of age don't understand exactly all that death involves. So you don't want to press on them something they are not ready to understand. But do answer what they are asking.

If a younger brother or sister asks you directly, "Am I going to die?" Dr. Easson recommends you answer, "We all die someday, but you are not going to die today or tomorrow." A young child has no concept of time like you do. Such a statement is the truth. But it is not too scary because it does not seem immediate.

In your answers, don't ever take away hope. And don't ever give up hope yourself. New drugs are discovered, new treatments are perfected, miracles are performed every day. We have all heard of cases which have astounded doctors beyond all belief. Faith and hope give courage to go on.

After everybody knows the situation, then what do you do? How do you live under such pressure? How do you treat a dying family member or friend? How can you help lighten their load and your own?

First, by understanding the emotions they and you are going through. When someone is told his time on earth is limited, he, as well as the family, begins a grieving process much like I described in chapter 3.

You may think that death is too scary or depressing for dying persons to talk about. But that's not the case at all. Dr. Kubler-Ross, working with dying people around the world, has discovered overwhelmingly that they *do* want to talk about their coming death. They do want to share feelings with family and friends. They need someone to listen and not pretend that life is going on as usual.

Let's examine the emotions of grief your ill loved one and you may experience and need to talk about.

The first reaction Dr. Kubler-Ross, in her book, *On Death and Dying*, calls denial. The person may refuse to believe that he's really sick. He may refuse to take medicine or treatments. He may talk a lot about what he's going to do ten years from now. You may talk about future plans without acknowledging your loved one may be gone. Denial is good at times in that it provides an escape from sadness. It's like a cover pulled over a child's head to protect him from the dark. You should never force a loved one to talk realistically. You both may need to deny from time to time to protect yourselves from pain.

The second reaction Dr. Kubler-Ross describes is anger. The sick one may be angry at the doctor for not having diagnosed the problem earlier or at the nurses for not taking better care of him. He may be angry at God for "letting this happen." He may be angry at himself for not going to the doctor sooner or not being more careful. He may be angry at another member of the family for "making him sick." He may be angry at the world—for being alive and happy when he's dying.

You may be angry at the huge expense the illness costs. It's not that you wouldn't give any amount of money to have your loved one well. But it seems a waste to see savings for a college education go down the drain when your loved one gets no better for all the money spent. Of course, even thinking about money in a time like this makes you feel guilty. And that guilt often turns to anger. You may be angry at the nurses for not coming around to check on your father enough. You may be angry at your classmates because they seem unconcerned that your brother is sick. All of these feelings of anger are normal. The very situation that life has to end for someone you love brings rage. Whether this anger is reasonable doesn't really matter. The anger is present.

Anger may grip the entire family. If your mother is hospitalized and your father gripes at you, it helps to know that really he is not angry with you—only the situation. He may not even realize where this anger is coming from. But knowing you're not the real cause can help you endure.

The third reaction is bargaining—an attempt to make a deal with God for a little more time on earth. A parent may promise to give a lot of money to a church or an orphanage if God will just let him live until you get out of school. A brother may bargain to be a preacher if God will just let him get through college. You may bargain to give your life as a missionary if God will just let your mother live. Even though this stage of bargaining is as real as the others, you and your family may not share these secret thoughts.

The fourth stage is depression. This is the time when the sick one finally realizes all the consequences of death. He or she is usually less active, untalkative, sad. A parent's thoughts center around all the events in the children's lives he or she will miss. The parent regrets the loneliness of his children. A father may worry about not leaving enough money for his family to manage on. You may be depressed thinking about specific events in the future like athletic performances, graduation, your wedding which your parent will never see. This is a time when families don't have much to say to each other. Instead, they help each other by just being together, hugging, and touching.

The final emotional stage is acceptance. This is when the dying person no longer denies he or she is sick and is neither angry or depressed. It's not a happy state—just one devoid of almost all feelings. The sick one will be tired, weak, untalkative, sleepy. This is his way of detaching his emotions from people he loves—to make it easier to die. He or she merely wants your presence.

You may resent this stage of acceptance, thinking your loved one is giving up, not trying anymore, deserting you. One girl said, "I hope when the end finally comes, I'm really feeling down and miserable, and that the world is a rotten place. That way I won't hate to leave it so much."

That's exactly what happens. Nature helps the dying person let go of his ties to people he loves. Your own pain will be lighter if you understand your loved one's acceptance of coming death.

These emotional stages or reactions don't always follow one

right after the other. Even after a sick person reaches the stage of depression, he may, for a day or two, deny that he is really sick.

And all these reactions do not occur in every person. Some people never get past the denial stage. Up until the time they die, they hang on to the idea that nothing is really wrong—that everything will eventually get better. Some people never get past the anger stage. They die shouting at everyone around them, finding nothing or no one to suit them.

Families, too, vary in their reactions. You may still feel angry at the time of your loved one's death. You may still try to deny that all this could really happen to you. On the other hand, you may have passed through all these feelings and have come to accept a death before it even occurs. This happens many times when the illness has been a long one. One boy said, "At my dad's funeral, I couldn't shed a tear. It was just like I had already cried so much in the five months he was sick that I didn't have any emotions left. Nothing." Again, this acceptance is nature's way of helping you separate emotionally and recover from your pain.

Whatever the situation facing you, it helps to understand your loved one's emotions, as well as your own. Expressing your deepest feelings to each other and knowing you're understood brings comfort to all involved.

Let's consider, now, more specific and practical questions and problems that come up when a family member is seriously ill.

Should you go about your normal routine? Should you go off on a weekend ski trip when your sister is in the hospital? Should you keep on working out every afternoon with the team or come on home to spend more time with your mother? These are normal questions and thoughts. You want to spend as much time as possible with your loved one, yet you have to go on living. You have to plan ahead, to live your own life.

It is usually best to keep as close to your normal routine as possible. For the sick one's benefit, as well as your own. The sick person feels guilty when the rest of the family has to plan their lives around him. Being a burden on others is one of the greatest fears of dying persons. So, don't make unnecessary schedule changes and cancel all social plans. You can't be with your family continually; you need to get away from the sadness from time to time.

Should you tell outsiders about the illness? It may be easier on you for others to know because you won't have to pretend. You can express your true feelings and explain your depression or sadness from time to time. On the other hand, you may not want to tell people for fear they will withdraw because of their own fears of death. You may feel that people will think you're using the situation to gain an unfair advantage—to gain a teacher's sympathy and get a good grade. To tell or not to tell outsiders, then, is an individual decision. Discuss it with your family and do whatever makes you most comfortable.

Should you let your loved one talk about approaching death? Overwhelmingly, professionals and patients agree that this is a tremendous help. Almost always, the sick person wants to talk about his fears and feelings of possible death.

That means you have to be willing to listen. And that's a big order. When your father starts talking about how he wants you to handle your college money, you may want to run from the room. When your brother says he wants you to have his stereo when he "no longer needs it," you may want to shut off his words with "don't talk like that." But do your best to listen; let your loved one prepare and express his wishes. It gives a parent great comfort to know that he is doing all he can to take care of your needs even after he or she is gone. Listen to what he or she needs to express.

A loved one may tell jokes or talk in a light way about his appearance, his treatment, or his coming death. Although painful to you, try to understand and not be shocked. Such talk may be his way of making the pain lighter for himself.

Even though the sick one wants you to listen and to let him express his deepest thoughts, at times he will withdraw. A brother or sister may want to talk in the morning before school. By afternoon, he or she may ignore serious comments or questions you have. Try to understand both his need to talk and his need to be quiet. A dying person has mood changes like everyone else. Be sensitive to his or her needs.

Don't be afraid to tease or "be happy" around your loved one. Talk about routine things in a normal way as much as possible. The sick one can see that life is going on around him and that he is not "depressing" everyone. To see everyone sad would make him feel like a burden and unwanted.

Here are some other things you can do to help: If one parent is in the hospital and the other is having to be gone a lot, the younger kids in the family may feel neglected and scared. You can devote more time to talking and playing with them. Nurses even use what they call "play therapy" to help young children adjust to a death situation. You may help a sister or brother express his feelings about death through his playing. If he draws a picture of a house or a family, take time to let him tell you about his picture. He may be trying to mention some fear or question he has.

If it's a younger brother or sister who's ill, of course you'll want to spend extra time with him or her. You may even want to babysit for an entire weekend to give your parents a break from the daily strain. You may occasionally drive the brother or sister to the treatment center to help your parent out. Sometimes you can help by being extra tolerant when a sick brother uses his illness to manipulate or get his way unfairly.

But you may catch yourself feeling resentful instead of wanting to help. Such feeling is normal. A sick sister takes your parents' time and attention from you. And it is very difficult to always have to plan meals, outings, shopping trips, or homework projects around treatment schedules. Be as tolerant as possible, but try not to feel guilty when resentment creeps in.

Another special problem is being afraid of an emergency situation when you are alone at home with the sick one. You may be afraid to be left alone because his or her condition may take an unexpected turn for the worse. You can ease your fear by making sure you have discussed beforehand what to do in case of emergencies. You should have the doctor's telephone numbers handy. Know which neighbor or friend to call for help at particular times of the day in an immediate crisis. Encourage other family members to make a habit of always leaving word where they'll be when they go off for several hours. However, when the sick one is ill enough to warrant this fear, he or she is usually hospitalized rather than at home.

Another fear is seeing the sick one's physical appearance change. Drugs and treatments may cause scars, swelling, weight gain or loss, baldness. This can be one of the most horrifying things you experience—seeing someone you love endure these physical changes. But staying away from the hospital can be worse than seeing the person because your mind often imagines things worse than reality.

Another thing you will have to participate in and help plan is the funeral. Of course, you won't be responsible for handling the majority of the details. But you will probably be asked about your opinions. At the immediate time of death, it is difficult to think about the funeral and know what you should do. That's why some parents who know they are dying discuss their funeral arrangements with the family ahead of time. That is another time when you may need to listen, as a comfort to your parent, even when you're hurting.

It is not at all uncommon in this day and time to discover that many young people have never attended a funeral. Many would agree that this is a recent effort of our culture to deny the reality of death—to think that science has almost conquered all. If you have never been to a funeral, you may be fearful about what to expect.

Funerals are conducted differently by different ministers of different religious groups. But, primarily, a funeral contains the same parts: a eulogy (good comments about the dead one's life), comforting Scriptures passages and prayers for the family's adjustment to the loss, a short sermon or talk by the minister. In the sermon he may give a challenge to the congregation to live a life which exemplifies the most important things in life. Or, he may encourage the audience to make spiritual preparation for their own deaths.

During the service, the family members sit together in a designated place in the funeral home or the church. The coffin is placed either at the front or the back of the church. At the end of the service, the congregation and family members may or may not (depending on what the family has decided beforehand) pass by the coffin on the way out of the building. The family, congregation, pall bearers (people who carry the coffin), and funeral directors accompany the coffin to the burial place. There, the minister may again say a few words or read a passage of Scripture before the loved one's body is buried.

The funeral is a part of the healing process—as I mentioned in chapter 3. Attending a funeral helps you realize the reality of the situation and helps you work through the pain more quickly. Most counselors agree that anyone seven or older should be encouraged to attend the funeral. If you have a younger brother or sister, encourage your parent to permit them to attend the funeral. Otherwise, children feel isolated and alone with their grief. Despite the ages of a younger brother or sister, don't shut them away from you physically or emotionally. Support and love each other in working through your pain during the immediate time of the funeral and burial.

So far, I've been talking about facing a terminal illness in your own family—a sick parent, grandparent, brother, or sister. In helping a seriously ill friend, most of these ways to help still apply. But other special concerns come up in this relationship.

If the ill one is a very close friend, you probably still visit often. But visiting may be difficult for you. Many dying teens complain that friends seem to pull away and gradually quit coming around.

Examine your own feelings to see if and why you may be pulling away from a sick friend. You may be pulling away because you fear death. This is natural. Death makes you feel insecure—that you, too, may die. Just at a time when you are becoming independent from your parents and can manage many decisions and problems on your own, death rears its head and makes you realize you need other people.

Another reason for hesitating to be around a sick friend is his or her physical condition. Although a friend's appearance may be changed and upsetting, he is still the same person on the inside. He needs your visit, your love, your support.

You may be hesitant to visit because you are afraid of the illness. Doctors say that many people have a special fear about cancer—the most fatal disease of young people. Dr. Jan van Eys, of the M. D. Anderson Hospital which deals exclusively with cancer patients, says people seem to be very prejudiced about cancer, as if afraid they would catch it. Cancer is not contagious. This is a prejudice to overcome.

Another reason—a selfish one—why some teens withdraw from sick friends is that they have no future. If you are hesitant to be around a sick friend, ask yourself if possibly you have "written off" someone because they won't be around to experience the things you are planning. Even though that friend accepts the reality that his time is limited, he still wants to know what life is like for other people. He still needs to be part of others' lives.

After examining your own feelings, you may have uncovered some hesitancy on your part about being with your ill friend. Although this feeling is understandable, it is something to work at overcoming. A mature person learns to control his own fears in such a way as to reach out to other people when they need help.

On the other hand, you may genuinely want to be with your friend. But what to do or say around him or her?

One teen answers this way: "Just talk to me like we were at home. But I don't like it when everybody comes in big groups and just stands around and stares at you, you know. I want them to sit down, sit on the bed, just talk about what they've been up to. Normally, I like to tell what they've been doing to me. You know—the nurses did this or that and I have to take these pills. Just normal stuff. Just talk about any little thing."

But what about when you run out of "just normal stuff"? Maybe you're at a loss about what to ask your sick friend. But even hospitals have daily routines. You can ask what the patient's daily schedule is, how the food is, what the rest of his family is doing, about hobbies, or TV programs. Ask questions and then really listen to what your friend has to say. You can always share your big interests of the moment. Certainly, your friend will have the time to become really involved in what you're saying and feeling.

Naturally, if you can, cheer the person up. Another patient describes a special girlfriend's visit: "This one girl came to see me this time. She was dressed like a clown. I mean the whole get-up—the nose, the rosy cheeks. She was just darling. And she brought this huge, huge box. And way, way down in the bottom, there was this stuffed bunny. I mean that meant so much to me. Just that little thing. For her to go to that much trouble. I mean you don't have to take everybody in the hospital a present. But something like that made me know somebody was thinking about me."

However, your friend won't always need you to cheer him up. Sometimes he or she will just need you to be around in the sad times. Try to fit into whatever mood your friend happens to be in. If he wants to talk seriously, be a good listener—even if what he or she says is painful or scary to you.

Don't let tears upset you. I've already mentioned that tears are a release and good for the individual. If your friend or you cries, what does it matter? Tears mean that you love deeply and are saddened by the situation.

What if the friend is bitter and asks you why this is happening? You are not expected to have answers—answers to why this illness is happening, why he has to go through painful treatments, why anything. Just listen with a caring attitude.

What about discussing religious matters? If your friend and you are Christians, it will probably be natural to talk from time to time about matters of religion—share opinions about God and what happens after death.

If your friend is not a Christian, certainly this is a time when he's seeking answers about his destiny after death. You might share your faith by first asking your friend about his own views and religious background. You might ask him if he attends any church. Then, after listening to his answers, you might share things about your religious background, telling him that you go to such-and-such church. Then proceed to share the period in your life when you first decided you needed to make a personal commitment to Jesus Christ and began to know God in a personal way.

Ask what sort of concept of God he has. If your friend seems interested in talking further, explain how he can invite Jesus into his life. Or, you might want to suggest and arrange a meeting with another Christian friend or pastor who can explain how he could become a Christian.

If your friend is bitter over his illness, don't preach to him about his attitude. God can "defend" himself, reveal himself to your friend, and love him even when there is anger and frustration about dying. Don't feel that you must have all the answers to why God permits things. Listen to what the friend says and offer your love in spite of the bitterness. God may have another time or way for you to share your faith with that friend.

Don't make promises like "God has told me that he is going to heal you." This type reassurance from friends is common because people want to offer hope. But statements like that can be very upsetting to the friend and his family. If God is going to perform a miracle in that person's life such as allowing a new drug or treatment discovery, God will let that friend and family know. If God does not perform a miracle, such statements bring disappointment and more pain.

Finally, no matter the response to your sharing, offer your support, love, hope, and confidence in God's control of the situation.

What about the sick friend's family? Don't forget they are going through the same grieving process as the sick one. From time to time, ask them how they feel, how they're managing. Ask about other things besides the illness. They need a release and an opportunity to talk about other interests, too.

And don't forget other specific, practical ways you can help. Offer to run errands, baby-sit with younger kids in the family, drive your friend back and forth to the hospital for treatments—whatever the situation calls for.

Last, you may need to be a family mediator. At the beginning of the chapter, I talked about the importance of being open and honest about the possibility of approaching death. That is very difficult for some families. As a result, your friend and his family may be together physically, but emotionally isolated. The family may be desperate to express their feelings; the sick friend may be desperate to talk and prepare mentally for his death. Yet, tragically, they remain silent about the deepest pain of their lives.

You may be the necessary instrument in bringing them together. It may only be necessary for you to say something like, "Mrs. White, Janet really seems to want to talk about her illness and how she is feeling about what's ahead. She's talked about it to me several times. I think she'd like to discuss it with you, too, but doesn't know how to bring it up or want to upset you."

Or, to your friend you might need to suggest, "Why don't you tell your mother about how much you're afraid of losing your hair? She might find out some things you can do about it until it grows back." Or, "Why don't you ask your dad about his beliefs about afterlife?"

Such brief statements just may be the encouragement the friend and parent needs to bridge the gap of isolation.

Facing up to a fatal illness and approaching death of either a family member or a friend requires great maturity and emotional strength. We have been conditioned in our culture to deny death, to turn in the opposite direction. But dying persons need your love and your presence.

Won't you be the one to help them in their time of deepest loneliness?

Every one can master a grief but he that hath it.
Shakespeare

5
Helping a Friend Handle Grief

Have you ever had a friend help you with a project and be more in the way than a help? It's not that you didn't appreciate the friend's intentions; it's just that you could have done the job better on your own. Such might be the case with a grieving friend. Even though your friend will appreciate your good intentions, there are some better and best ways to help.

One "best" way you can help is simply with your presence. Your just being around says, "I care." When you are at a loss for words, touching—a handshake or an embrace—is the most fundamental form of communicating.

The first time you are together after your friend's loss, you can say something like, "I came by to say how sorry I am about your father." From that statement on, you can follow the friend's lead about what he needs or wants to talk about. Don't be afraid of tears your words or your visit may bring. If tears begin, don't quit talking, change the subject, or leave. Instead, listen to what the friend says despite his tears. He needs and wants to talk about his loss.

Talk about the one who has died. The grieving friend wants to talk about his loss. It's his way of memorializing the dead one and saying "I love you" to that person one last time. You can say good things about the person such as, "Your brother was really friendly; I remember how he went out of his way to speak to me when . . . ." Or, "Your mother was really a sweet person, I remember the day she . . . ." To a dead friend's parent you might say, "Our team is sure going to miss Pat; he always kept our fighting spirit up for the games."

If you didn't know the dead one well, you can say something like: "I didn't know Mark very well, but from what you told me (or from what others have said), he must have really been a fun person (or considerate, or talented, or whatever)." These statements encourage your friend to express his own feelings about the person and to share meaningful times they've had together. By helping your friend praise and remember his loved one, you show that you really understand his loss.

But remember that everyone has moods and goes through different stages of mourning at his own pace. So, if for some reason your friend does not want to talk, you can sense that. Unless you know the friend very well, stay only a short time—about ten or fifteen minutes. Your coming has said that you care and want to be of help. You might tell him or her what you are available to do in the way of specific help (things I'll mention later), and call or come back later.

Sometimes you see the friend out on the street after a recent death, and you realize you haven't expressed sympathy in any way. Maybe he or she is just a casual acquaintance and you only know about the death secondhand.

You may be reluctant to say something about the death while you're out in public because he or she may break down and cry. On the other hand, you feel you should say something. It is usually good to make some sort of comment such as "I was sorry to hear about your father. How are you getting along now?" Or, "I heard about your brother's accident. I'm sorry . . . . Do you still have relatives visiting?" Or, "Have you caught up with your schoolwork yet?" After their answer, go on to another subject.

Usually such a slight, sympathetic comment will not bring

tears. (Not that causing tears is bad, only that the time or place may be embarrassing for that person.) Yet, such a statement is a courtesy. It would be rather coldhearted not to say anything.

Grieving persons can become very bitter toward friends who fail to mention the death at all. They don't realize that you do care but are just unsure about what to say. So it is best to acknowledge that you are sorry in some way.

If the grieving person is a close friend, however, you'll be around them to share their grief in a much deeper way.

The first thing to remember in trying to help is not to judge another's grief reactions—attitudes and behavior. If you've been through a similar situation, it's easy to compare your friend's feelings to your own. But remember what I said in chapter 3 about everyone expressing grief in his own way. One person may be silent; another very talkative. One may be angry at himself, the doctors, or another family member; another may not be angry at all. Try to understand your friend's thoughts, feelings, and wishes without coloring them to suit yourself. The most important thing to remember is that the grieving person wants to talk.

Your job is to listen.

You remember the grief stages I described in chapters 3 and 4—denial, anger, bargaining, depression, and acceptance. Your friend will have to work through most of these emotions to get relief from his pain. You can help him or her get through the denial stage by helping him face reality. No matter how much you may want to protect your friend from the hurt, that is not possible. If he is to be healed from the wound of loss, he has to work through the pain—not cover it up.

To help him or her begin the adjustment, don't encourage sedatives—pills or words. Sometimes family members ask their doctors for medicine to put them to sleep or numb them after such a great loss. Most professionals, however, agree that taking

HELPING A FRIEND HANDLE GRIEF

sedatives only delays adjustment to the loss. Of course, only with a close friend will you be in a position to say anything about whether your friend should take pills. But if asked, you can encourage him or her not to.

Words can also become sedatives, as Dr. Jackson in *Understanding Grief*, points out. Reassurances that everything will be all right and that everything is under control can be sedatives in that they help your friend continue to deny the reality of death. Your assurances may keep your friend from thinking about his loss. He must face the consequences of the death and work through it.

Another thing you can do to help your friend through the denial stage is to encourage him to attend the funeral of the loved one. Most friends of teen age or older will want to attend. But in certain circumstances, your friend may be hesitant to do so. Again this is a form of denying and refusing to face up to reality. You should encourage your friend to view the body of his loved one to help him get on with working through his pain.

If and when your friend passes through the anger stage, you will need to show special understanding and tolerance. The friend may be angry at the one who died for leaving them alone, angry at other kids who still have parents, angry at himself for not having been able "to do something" to prevent the death. You may be able to break through any anger caused by guilt by reminding the friend of good things he said or did for his loved one.

The grieving friend may express anger toward you. Leah's best friend, Karen, died in an automobile accident. Leah thought that being with Karen's older sister, Christy, and sharing how much she loved her friend would be a comfort. But Christy was cold and distant toward her. When Leah stopped by the friend's house, Christy seemed too busy to stop and talk like she used to do. Leah's appearance and disposition made Christy think too much of her sister. She was subconsciously angry that Leah could go on living and her own sister had died unfairly. Such a reaction is irrational, but not uncommon.

The friend may be angry at God. He or she may keep asking. "Why did God let this happen?" Don't try to shut a friend up when he or she expresses anger at God. God does not need a defender at such times. He is powerful enough to take care of his own reputation and to bring understanding to a person's mind at the proper time.

Don't feel that you have to answer a friend's questions about why the death happened. Most people don't expect answers. And that's good, because no one has the answers for every case. At such a time when the friend is angry, just listen to his or her questions, doubts, fears. Say, "I don't know," or, "I can't understand it either." Your friend just needs to express his hurt and puzzlement. God will give understanding in his own way and time.

Don't ever imply or hint that the death is a punishment for something. People already feel guilty enough for many real or imagined reasons. Don't add to their pain by hinting that this death may be God's way of "shaping them or somebody else up."

In a few days, when the person has passed through this anger, then is the time to share your faith in God's plan and his goodness. At that time they are in a more receptive mood and can hear you. Then share your beliefs, in an afterlife and try to comfort the person.

As your friend continues to pass through the emotions of grief, here are some other specific things to avoid saying:

Don't tell your friend not to worry. Such a comment sounds like you are ignoring the situation. When a friend's parent dies, his problems may seem insurmountable—finances, his future education, a possible move, missed schoolwork. To ignore the problems and give a pat answer like, "Everything will all work out," makes the person think you are not really understanding his predicament. And such a comment is sometimes taken as, "Chin up, you're not the only person with problems. A lot of people face death." The friend may feel like you're saying his loss is just another statistic.

Don't tell the friend your own problems. The friend's emotional circuits are already overloaded. He or she can't bear to think about other problems. You may think that by telling your own problems you will help him unload his own. But at this particular time, that is not the case. At such times, unloading your problems may come across at, "Don't tell me your troubles, I've got enough of my own." Listen to your friend's situation; you can share your problems later or with another friend for the time being.

Don't say, "Call me if you need anything," or, "Let me know if I can help." Such offers are too broad. Many people are insincere when they make such general statements. The friend needing help doesn't know if you really mean what you say. And even if he does sense your sincerity, he doesn't know to what extent you're willing to help. For instance, are you willing to give up a Friday night date to do something for them? Are you willing to spend some money? Are you willing to take time off from your after-school job? You see how that statement can be an empty offer.

And even if the friend knows you're sincere and that you'd do anything he might ask, he may not know what needs to be done. He is in a painful, sometimes numbed, state and really may not be thinking clearly.

Now that I've mentioned some things not to do or say, let's move on to positive suggestions for helping:

Deliver messages. You may need to tell your friend's teachers at school why he is absent and arrange for keeping up with his missed assignments. You may need to call other school friends who are not aware of the death so that they can express their sympathy by a card or attending the funeral. You may need to call the coach to tell him why your friend won't be at the game.

Run errands. Your friend may need you to take or pick up clothes from the cleaners which he or she wants to wear to the funeral. You may need to go buy some shampoo or a new tie before the friend has to leave town.

Buy or cook food to take to the family. Most families have relatives who come to stay for a few days at the time of death. They need extra food at a time when no one feels like cooking. You may want to prepare a casserole to take by the house. Or, if you don't know how to cook, you may want to go by a bakery or delicatessen and buy food to take.

Baby-sit. If the family and relatives have very small children, they may need someone to baby-sit during the funeral. Or, they may need baby-sitting help both before and after the funeral while so many arrangements and details need to be taken care of.

Help clean up your friend's room. Most people are not overly concerned with an immaculate house at the time of death. But most would probably feel better if the house or their room was fairly straightened up before guests and relatives began arriving. This would be a good way to "be with" your friend and also do something practical while there. Or, ask for the house key and clean while the family is away at the funeral home.

Help with schoolwork. Most kids will miss a few days to a few weeks of school due to an extended illness or death. You can arrange to get all their assignments while they're gone. If you are in the same class and know the material, you can offer explanations when your friend begins the makeup work. Even if you don't know anything about the assignments, offer to collect library materials for an assigned report or to type a paper.

I'm sure that with each individual situation you can add many other ways to help. The important thing to remember is to be specific with offers. Don't just exit with a "let-me-know-if-there's-anything-I-can-do" statement.

Remember what I said about a friend's help not really being help at all? It's always a good idea to mention what you can do and make sure it's OK with your friend—that he really wants or needs that specific thing done.

All these things primarily relate to the time of intense pain immediately after a death. But even though your friend's pain seems to subside after a few days or weeks, he or she is not through the grieving process in such a short time.

You need to keep on caring. Ask frequently how the person is feeling or provide ways for the friend to mention his loss and talk about the one who has died. The friend wants to keep that grandparent, parent, brother or sister's memory alive. Don't be afraid to make statements like, "Your mother would have really enjoyed this movie." Even though such a comment may bring tears, that's OK. Such a remark is a tribute and says to the friend that you still remember the mother's personality.

Keep on caring by making an extra effort to be with that friend more. Help him pick up his usual routine. Most cultures have a certain mourning period. During this time the family remains alone and avoids social activities out of respect for the dead. But in our culture, no such specific mourning time is set aside. A friend may want to go out to a movie or ride around with friends just to forget his pain for a few hours. But he or she may feel others will condemn them for being "disrespectful" or "thoughtless." So, each person will feel differently about when and if he should resume his normal school and social routine. You'll just have to be sensitive to what you think your friend feels and needs.

If you're unsure, you can ask something like, "Do you feel like seeing a movie with us next weekend?" You are showing that you still remember his loss, but are offering to help him forget for awhile and gain some release from loneliness. If your friend doesn't want to go out yet, just go to his house and hang around. Just having someone "there" can be a great comfort.

The best thing you can do for a friend who has recently lost someone he loves is to share your faith in God. That does *not* mean "preaching" or even talking to him or her about religious beliefs at the immediate time of death. I mentioned earlier the hazards of discussing your faith at a time when the friend may be angry or questioning why the death has happened. But a week, two weeks, a month later, when the initial pain has subsided—then is the time to share your faith in God and encourage that friend who is not a Christian to make a commitment to him.

Of course, if your friend does not seem angry or bitter, you can share your Christian beliefs at a much earlier time and bring comfort by discussing your confidence in God's provision for that loved one in heaven.

Sometimes to help a person, you may need to realize when you *can't* help. That may sound strange, but many people want to help a friend so badly that sometimes they don't realize their own limitations. You may run into situations when your friend is behaving abnormally—so much so that you need to encourage him or her to get professional help. And you may be the only person close enough to recognize such a situation. Dr. Erich Lindemann, former professor of psychiatry at Harvard University, has compiled a list of "abnormal" reactions to grief. These may help you identify a friend's need for outside help:

1. When a person is overactive and seems to be feeling "on top of the world" rather than feeling a loss and sadness.

2. When the person starts complaining with imagined symptoms of the same illness of which the loved one just died.

3. When the person actually develops an illness caused by intense emotional stress such as ulcers or migraine headaches.

4. When the person shows a complete change in his behavior toward all his family and friends.

5. When the person is furiously angry or hostile toward specific people who he thinks had something to do with the death.

6. When the person acts like he's just going through the motions of living without any feelings.

7. When the person completely gives up his old patterns of relationships with friends and acts restless.

8. When the person begins to do things harmful to his own welfare—like giving away all his possessions or quitting school.

9. When the person seems severely depressed.

Remember that normal reactions include shock or numbness, anger, and depression. The above list of "warning signals" refers to reactions that hang on for a long time and don't seem to be disappearing.

If you recognize one or more of these problems in your friend, encourage him or her to get professional help in making an adjustment to the loss. Encourage the friend to talk to the school counselor or to a minister. Or encourage him to call a mental health clinic listed with county, state, or federal government agencies in the telephone directory. The agency can arrange for your friend to get help for whatever his family can afford to pay—free, if necessary.

Helping a friend in time of grief can be one of the most difficult and one of the most rewarding things you'll ever do. Helping someone else strengthens your own inner resources for such a crisis. To give is to receive.

The miserablest day we live there is many a better thing to do than die.
George Darley

6
Psychological First Aid for Suicidal Friends

The bell sounded to dismiss class. Picking up an armload of books, I dashed out the front door into the bright sunlight. A patrol car in the parking lot caught my attention. A ticket? For what?

As I got closer, I could see no yellow or pink slip of paper flapping under the windshield wiper. Another patrol car stopped in the next aisle and two more officers came toward the area. Students and administrators headed toward my car from different angles of the campus. What was going on?

Fumbling to get out my keys, I rounded the front of my car. Then I saw it. A heap of white sheets lying on the pavement in between the two cars next to mine.

An approaching voice asked, "What happened?"

The answer came back from somewhere, "Girl just shot herself."

I got in my car shakily; I felt sick to my stomach. Somebody had just shot herself right beside where I was sitting. Here. Five minutes ago. It was like a slap in the face. Suicide. Why?

The next day as student after student entered my classroom, the first question was, "Did you hear what happened?" followed by details. The student had walked out to the parking lot after her last class of the day, pulled a gun from her purse, and shot herself through the head. She'd left in her notebook notes to each teacher. The notes simply said that she was killing herself because no one cared. My class talked on and on about how someone should have known and helped.

Then Katrina walked in, her face drawn, her black eyes hard and angry. She took her usual seat by the window and stared around the room without joining in the conversation.

The bell sounded and I called the class to order. "I believe Katrina is to read her work first today," I said.

Katrina pulled out her yellow note pad and began to read: "This is not a short story. This is what I wrote throughout the night of October 9." She continued to read her own reconstruction of the suicide scene. She had left the school building a few minutes earlier than I had and had been the one to discover the body and call the police. She continued to read: "Seeing that body and realizing what had happened brought back all the horrors and feelings I experienced a few years ago when my own father killed himself . . . ."

The class sat motionless as she read. Anger, rejection, sympathy, understanding, hate, love, revulsion, shame, guilt, pain were all poured out as she read her description of the intense emotional pain she'd gone through at the time of her father's death and then again when she walked up to the girl's suicide scene. As she finished reading thirty-five minutes later, no one could speak.

Katrina, herself, finally broke the silence again, "I'm sorry if I've depressed everybody. But I had to write that and get it out of my system. You don't know what I went through last night. Seeing that girl brought back all those memories."

Depressing, unpleasant, scary. Yet, we must come to terms with suicide and learn how to prevent it. Chances are great that you will know someone who attempts or commits suicide sometime during his or her teen years. Suicide is the third leading cause of death for fifteen- to twenty-four-year-olds, third only to accidents and homicides. That means nearly five thousand young people commit suicide each year, an average of thirteen per day. And researchers tell us that triple that number may be more accurate because suicides are often labeled accidents. What's more, the rate is rapidly increasing.

So what can you do about it? Dr. Calvin J. Frederick with the National Institute of Mental Health says our biggest prevention measure is teaching "psychological first aid" to other teens and to adults who work with teens. Learning "psychological first aid" simply means to know how to help others through their emotional crises.

First, you need a basic understanding about suicide. Here are some un-facts, thought true in the past, but which have now been proven incorrect.

People who try to kill themselves are mentally ill. Not true. The fact is that most suicides are impulsive. The period of depression which leads to the suicide is brief. The act is not something that's been planned and thought about for a long time. "Normal" teens kill themselves.

People who talk about killing themselves never do. Not true. People who talk about killing themselves are giving out clues and asking for help. If they don't get it, statistics tell us they will follow through.

Suicide runs in the family. Not true. Suicide is not hereditary. But a person's belief that it is tends to make him more susceptible to the urge when depression hits.

If all these are un-facts about suicide, then what is true? Suicides are often called attacks—attacks against the person himself, against another person, against society.

With this basic understanding of suicide, professionals have come up with several main reasons why teens kill themselves.

Competition. Teens may feel stress over competition for grades, athletics, or future jobs. The teen's suicide may be an attack against himself because he feels inadequate, frustrated, or ashamed. It may be an attack against someone he feels is pressuring him to compete. It may be an attack against society in general because society fosters competition and makes him feel inadequate.

Divorce. A teen may be upset by the absence of one parent or scared of the new living arrangement. He may think he caused some of the marriage problems and may feel guilty. His suicide may be his way of punishing himself or punishing his parents for their divorce.

Moving. A teen may be lonely, frustrated, and unhappy within himself because he can't adjust to a new place. Or, he may kill himself to punish his parents for moving. Or, the suicide may be directed toward others—the school, club, or church kids who won't let him into their group.

Shame, fear, guilt. A teen may kill himself to punish himself for something he's done which he considers "unforgivable." He may feel guilty about the pain he's caused others. He may fear having to adjust to some new situation or pressure.

Rejection. A teen may kill himself because he feels no one needs or loves him. If he agrees that he's worthless, the suicide is self-punishment. Or, his death may be to "get even" with someone who has turned away from him—a boyfriend, girlfriend, parent. Or, he may think that all of society has rejected him; his suicide is an attack against everyone.

Adolescence. This may seem strange as a cause. But Jacques Choron, in his studies, found that some stresses which just come with being a teenager may lead to suicide—new sex drives, awkward coordination, severe acne. "What everybody thinks" is vitally important to most teens. Because everything seems geared to "right now," some teens don't have the patience to hang around until things change for the better. Their whole future gets out of perspective.

Purposelessness. From the age of about ten, people begin to search for a purpose in life—a reason to be on earth, goals to make their life meaningful. This is instinctive. People who don't have a purpose may kill themselves as an attack on the rest of the human race which has left them out. Or, their suicide may be an attack on themselves because they can't seem to find their niche.

A wish for reunion. Some persons kill themselves because they wish to be reunited with a dead loved one.

Now, with this basic understanding of suicide facts and reasons, let's move on to learning "psychological first aid."

First, train yourself to pick up clues of dangerous situations. The most obvious clue is hinting or threatening statements. "You'd be better off without me." "I won't be around much longer." "If something happened to me, they'd sure be sorry." "How many pills do you think it'd take to kill someone?"

Also, be aware of clues in a friend's behavior:

1. Someone who is habitually absent from school.
2. Someone who doesn't get along with his family and who has run away or is considering running away.
3. Someone who is always in trouble at school and can't get along with adults.
4. Someone who is on drugs or alcohol.
5. Someone who seems extremely bored with life and wants to be alone and do nothing.
6. Someone whose grades have taken a sudden, unexplained decline.
7. Someone who has gone through a particularly emotionally upsetting situation like divorce of their parents, moving, a death.
8. Someone who shows some of these physical symptoms: loss of appetite, trouble sleeping at night, bursting into tears easily, no energy, neglected appearance.

Besides these on-the-surface clues of potential suicide victims, numerous counselors claim that reckless driving, drinking, smoking, provoking others to a physical fight, or taking other unnecessary risks are hidden wishes to die.

Of course, none of these symptoms alone mean that someone is considering or might consider suicide. But these are flashing red lights. When there is *any* drastic change in someone's behavior, consider it a signal for help.

To administer "psychological first aid" in these situations, then, be alert. Stay tuned in to people around you. Listen to their cries for help before they become desperate. Don't make anyone you know go to such extremes to get your attention.

Second, be a friend. Show the person you really care, that you accept what he or she is, that you want to understand and help. A caring attitude is the most important thing in persuading someone to live.

Third, talk to him or her about the problem. Try to discover the real cause of his depression and then help him find solutions.

For instance, here is a sample dialogue to show you how you might help a friend find a solution:

You: You seem really down. Can you tell me what's the matter? Maybe I can help.

Friend: You can't. It's school and my parents. I'm flunking.

You: Have you had trouble before?

Friend: Yeah. Algebra. Last year.

You: What happened then?

Friend: My parents had a fit and grounded me for a month.

You: Then what happened?

Friend: I finally got this neighbor's older son to help me study for the final exam.

You: Could you do that again?

Friend: No. He moved.

You: Well, tutoring helped. Let's go to the school counselor and ask if he'll recommend someone to tutor you before or after school. Some teachers give them extra points for that.

Notice that you have to ask questions and really care about his feelings. And you need to understand the details of the situation so you can suggest good solutions. Often the friend knows how he's solved the problem in the past, but just is discouraged this time.

After you hit upon a possible solution, encourage your friend to dwell on the times he's gone through a similar problem and has "come through" OK. Assure him that this problem can be handled, too, one way or another.

Give him a reason to want to overcome the problem. To discover what still matters to him, ask things like: Does your boyfriend know about this? What do you think he would say? Do you still want to be on the football team? Wouldn't you still like to learn to fly a plane? Don't you still want to be a veterinarian?

Don't be put off if the person keeps saying "nobody cares" or "nothing matters anymore." Watch the friend's facial expression. See if there's not some spark of interest when you mention things or persons he values. Play upon those spots of hope to give him incentive to overcome his present crisis.

After you've been able to talk the person through the major crisis time, don't try to handle the problem alone. You cannot be with someone at all times; you aren't always perceptive to when he or she is "down"; and you can't always find the best solutions to his problems.

Encourage the person to go with you to talk to someone else. The kind of problem often determines who you should contact to help with the solution. Encourage your friend to get to know an adult you admire and think the friend could relate to. This is especially beneficial if your friend's problem centers around conflict with his own parents. You may contact another family member, a teacher, a school counselor, or a minister. Or, phone a mental health clinic listed in the telephone book under federal, state, county, or city agencies, or a suicide-prevention center. There are over 200 such centers in the United States and another 675 additional community health centers which have walk-in counseling services and call-in hotlines.

Fourth, even after the immediate crisis seems to be over, stay in contact with the person. Encourage him to become involved in some worthwhile project. Everyone feels better when he feels needed and can contribute something to society. The project may be something simple like tutoring a neighborhood kid or a daily visit to an elderly person. And, or course, school clubs and churches usually have several service projects under way. If none of these interest your friend, call a volunteer agency and ask about jobs. Many cities have such an agency listed under "Junior Volunteer Corp" or some such title. If no such listing is given, call a hospital, orphanage, nursing home, or day-care center and ask about volunteer work you and your friend could do together.

If you don't know a specific individual who is in danger of suicidal urges, you can work at helping other kids with problems by suggesting the following to teachers or school counselors: (1) Set up hotlines manned by students on a volunteer basis for crisis calls. (2) Suggest a study of mental health to be included in a health education course. (3) Establish a peer-counseling program. In such a program, interested student-counselor volunteers go through a screening by teachers and counselors to see that they are relatively stable themselves. Then these volunteers go through a brief training period in which they learn how to listen effectively, how to present possible solutions to problems, how to lead the troubled teen to other sources of information and help for his specific problem.

For more information about how to set up such a peer-counseling program in your school, talk to your school guidance counselor.

All three ideas have been effective in suicide prevention

in various schools across the country. Volunteer to your school counselor to help get such programs or services set up in your school.

The last thing to remember in dealing with those who are depressed or who are considering suicide is that you can't always help.

Like Emily, who wrote about her father's suicide, you may feel guilty if someone you know attempts or is successful in killing himself. But some people, like Richard Cory, give no clues to their inner feelings. And their outward situation looks equally satisfying—even tempting to imitate. Try not to blame yourself if you did not spot the trouble and could not prevent the suicide.

In administrating "psychological first aid," share your ultimate purpose for living. Maybe your friend, too, will see that gleam of sunshine and cherish the opportunity to live.

Care. Save a life today.

If a man die, shall he live again?
Job 14:14

7
Is There Really Life After Death?

Death, what then? That's a question often debated but seldom settled. Most people give one of three answers: (1) When you die, you die. Your body deteriorates and that's it. (2) Your body deteriorates but your spirit goes to another world somewhere. Eventually, everybody ends up at the same place. (3) Your body deteriorates and your spirit either goes to heaven or hell.

Who's right? Is there proof? Does your spirit (soul, consciousness, being, personality) live on after physical death? Let's think through the question, weigh the evidence, and come to some conclusions.

First, consider the opinion that there is *no* life after death. Some believe that there is no design to the universe or human life, that man evolved from a cosmic explosion, and that both body and spirit will cease to exist after death.

Those who hold this view may still believe in immortality. (Immortality means existing forever.) But this idea of immortality is limited. Many have termed it "social" immortality. In other words, they believe that a person lives on in others' memories. His values and influence are passed on to his children. Another aspect of "social" immortality is through a person's lasting contributions to society—a scholarship fund, a library, a hospital. Others claim bodily immortality in that a person's physical characteristics are passed on. A great-great-grandchild may have the family's pug nose.

Those who do not believe in an afterlife *may* or *may not* believe in the concept of God. Some view God as a "force" behind the universe. They may believe that he created the world and controls its overall destiny but that he is not concerned with individuals and does not intervene in everyday life. Others believe he is a personal God who cares about individuals in this life, but who ends all life at physical death. Others believe there is no afterlife or God.

Now, let's move to the other side of the question and examine beliefs that there is life after physical death.

Again, there are different views about how a spirit or soul exists. Reincarnation is the belief that the soul continues to be recycled, so to speak. The same soul exists over and over in many bodily forms on earth. One soul may live and die as a Chinese, then an Englishman, then a cat, then a rose.

Others believe that there is a soul which continues to live after the body's death but does not exist as an individual being. It merges with one gigantic "soul of the universe." This idea may be illustrated by a vast cloud of steam. This steam cloud would represent the "one soul." Periodically, a few drops of steam condense and form water droplets (individuals). At death, heat would cause the water droplets to turn back into steam and join the one big steam cloud again. In other words, individual spirits exist only on earth. At death, these spirits merge into one "being" without individuality.

Others who believe in afterlife, believe in the soul's individual existence. They believe the soul continues to hover over the earth and to interact in the lives of earthly beings. This spirit may protect, punish, or frighten people on earth.

Finally, there are those who believe the soul keeps its individual identity and exists in a spiritual world all its own. This area of spiritual existence is unknown to beings on earth.

To sum up, then, views about life after death vary widely: Some believe that there is no existence after physical death. Earthly life is all there is. They may believe in a person's immortality in others' memory or in physical works done for society. They may or may not believe in a God who created and controls the universe.

On the other side of the question: Some believe that the soul continues to exist forever. They may believe that the soul lives in many bodily forms on earth. Others believe the soul has one existence on this earth, then goes to a new existence in a spiritual world and retains its individuality. Some believe the soul loses its individuality and becomes part of a gigantic "one soul." People with these views may or may not believe in a God who created and controls the universe.

Back to the basic question. Is there life after death? A recent Gallup opinion poll shows that 69 percent of the people in the United States say yes, 31 percent say no. How can one know for sure? By examining the evidence. Let's do that now.

When is a person dead? When the heart stops? When brain waves cease? When the person can no longer sustain life on his own efforts? When machines cannot sustain his life? All of these questions about when death occurs have led to renewed investigation into afterlife.

Probably the best-known work has been done by Dr. Elisabeth Kubler-Ross, medical doctor and psychologist. She has worked with the dying for many years and has written several books on death and dying. Interviewing dying patients all over the world in an effort to understand their needs, she concludes, "Before I started working with dying patients, I did not believe in a life after death. I now do believe in a life after death, beyond a shadow of a doubt."

Pause for a moment and close your eyes. Try to imagine yourself dead—nonexistent. Can you? Dr. Kubler-Ross goes on to say that the reason it is so hard to even imagine your own death is that there is no such thing. The spirit or personality never dies.

A well-known psychiatrist, Dr. Raymond L. Moody, investigating the death experience, has come to similiar conclusions. After interviewing over 150 persons who have been revived after being pronounced clinically dead, he has recorded his findings. The people interviewed termed their experience many different ways: a "homecoming," an "awakening," a "graduating," a "transition from one state to another," an "entry to a higher state of consciousness or of being."

Whatever the term, they basically experienced these same physical and emotional happenings:

They all insisted that there was no way they could describe or convey the feelings about the experience. They all remembered floating outside their bodies and hearing the news of their "death"; remembered comments of others in the room and the attempts to revive them; experienced feelings of peace and quiet; heard a loud noise like thunder or a roar; passed through something like a long tunnel; remembered meeting others who had died; encountered a "being of light"; approached a border or limit such as a fence, a shore, a wall, beyond which they could not go, and saw a panoramic review of their past life. They all remembered "coming back"; they either felt as though they were "sent back" or wanted to come back to finish things on earth. They all experienced a change in their life-styles, values, and attitudes after returning to life. They claimed to be no longer afraid to die, and to have a new desire to love and gain knowledge.

All of the 150 persons interviewed have had their story corroborated in as many ways as possible. For instance, a person's description of the attempts to revive and recall of comments made in the room after supposed death have been checked out with medical personnel. Changes in life-style have been verified by family and friends. Any experience which could not be verified by others was not used in the investigation.

To conclude, then, about Moody's findings: All interviewees who previously said they had no religious beliefs before the near-death experience have come to believe in afterlife.

Moody does not claim he has "proven" afterlife because his interview sample was not large enough (only 150 cases) and the interviewees were all from one culture. He only concludes that his investigation has changed his life and that he believes in afterlife.

A third doctor, Dr. Maurice Rawlings, former Pentagon personal physician to the Joint Chiefs of Staff and later heart specialist at the Diagnostic Hospital in Chattanooga, Tennessee, has followed up the work of these two doctors. Having revived many patients who screamed that they were in hell or afraid to die, he became puzzled as to why none of these people Moody and Kubler-Ross interviewed spoke of the biblical concept of hell. So he set about to do more interviews of near-death experiences of his own patients. Those he interviewed described the same things as the two other doctors mentioned. But about half of these patients had some kind of vision of hell. The difference in his reports and the previous ones is that he interviewed people at the *immediate* time of their vision. Moody and Kubler-Ross' interviews took place from several days to several years after the "death." When Rawlings later went back to those who had screamed about hellish experiences while "dying," most of them could not recall what they had said earlier. Rawlings, then, theorizes that these people had blotted such bad memories from their mind. (Psychologists tell us that such is the case with many unpleasant memories.) Rawlings also suggests that the pleasant experience described by so many could be a "sorting ground." Obviously, they never reached final judgment because they were revived and came back to earth. So, Dr. Rawlings' work and conclusions support Moody and Kubler-Ross' work.

Of course, many criticize these doctors' interviews saying that such visions are just hallucinations caused by medicine, wishful thinking, or cultural training. To investigate these charges, then, Drs. Karlis Osis and Erlendur Haraldsson, with the American Society of Psychical Research, began a study.

They started out with the idea to gather information to support the medical, psychological, and cultural explanations for these "visions." They decided to interview 1,000 doctors and nurses of two cultures—the United States and India. They chose to interview doctors and nurses rather than patients to get a more objective view—to eliminate a patient's "adding" to his story. To avoid prejudiced medical personnel (those who already believed in life after death), they took a random sampling—every seventh intern out of an alphabetical list. They chose people from two countries and two religions (Christianity and Hinduism) to see how much a person's religion and culture colored his deathbed experience.

Here are some of the things they found:

1. Patients on hallucinating-type drugs had fewer visions than patients who had no medicine at all. And hallucinating patients had visions of this present world, not a future world.

2. Patients with illnesses which cause hallucinations had fewer afterlife visions than patients who had other diseases.

3. Patients' visions of heaven or hell were not what they expected or were "trained to see" from their religious beliefs.

4. Persons from both cultures and all religions described the same experiences. They merely used different terms. For instance, Hindus called the "being of light" one of their deities. Christians called it Jesus or an angel.

Drs. Osis and Haraldsson's conclusions? That neither medicine, nor psychological, nor cultural training can explain away deathbed visions. They conclude, "We feel that the total body of information makes possible a fact-based, rational, and therefore realistic belief in life after death."

My list could go on and on about others who have read about, heard about, or had deathbed visions. Again, this is not proof, but strong evidence.

In addition to the evidence of personal deathbed accounts, many great minds—Socrates, Plato, Aristotle (to name a few)—have believed in afterlife. Also, ancient cultures and all major religions have believed in some form of afterlife. It would seem that belief in afterlife is instinctive in man.

Personal accounts, investigative work of numerous doctors, ancient philosophers, all major religions—the evidence strongly suggests life after death.

For the Christian, the Bible is the evidence for this belief. Let's review what the Bible says about the existence of death, afterlife, heaven, hell, and judgment.

The Bible teaches that there is an afterlife in which the soul continues to be known as an individual being. The Bible teaches that heaven and hell are real places. Heaven is briefly described as a magnificent place of beauty, riches, and harmonious relationships between all men and God. Hell is briefly described as a place of burning fire, of physical and mental torment, and of alienation and isolation from all that is good. In some respects, the concept of heavenly joy or hellish torment may be experienced on earth, but not in comparison to the way they will be experienced after death.

About judgment, the Bible teaches that all men's eternal destiny will be decided according to decisions made in this earthly life. Those who have trusted in Jesus Christ will be rewarded with a heavenly existence for eternity. Those who have lived without thought of spiritual matters and have rejected God's offer of eternal life will go to hell.

Finally, the Bible teaches that God created the world and controls its everyday affairs and overall destiny. He loves each individual and offers eternal life to all who accept his Son.

How do the writings of some of the other philosophers and present-day doctors measure up?

You can examine the difference in religious views about afterlife for yourself. But determining how present-day deathbed experiences measure up is more difficult. Primarily, the writings about near-death experiences have been attacked for two reasons. (1) Few people have told of visions of hell. (2) All have seemed to experience the same things—whether Christian or not.

To answer the first charge: That few recall experiences of hell can be explained by the fact that few people would tell of or be able to recall such painful memories. As mentioned earlier, the human mind blots out extremely painful experiences.

Second, obviously no one experienced final judgment because their "death" was not permanent. If you recall, all the interviewees saw something like a panoramic review of their past life. At this time, they had insights about the good and bad done in this life. But that does not necessarily conflict with the biblical idea that God will be the final Judge. In fact, that these people "came back to life" indicates that they never reached the final judgment time.

With the Bible as the measuring stick, then, we can say that recent studies verify, not question, the Bible.

If there is an afterlife, then, how do you prepare? How do you determine where you will spend the eternity of your existence?

The first step is to recognize you have a spiritual nature. Although people have no doubt about their physical existence, they sometimes have trouble understanding or "seeing" their spiritual nature. You see what you've been trained to see. For instance, if you and your family were to drive through a new city, chances are that each of you would notice different things. After the trip, your mother might comment on the azaleas blooming in every yard. You may not have even noticed the

IS THERE REALLY LIFE AFTER DEATH? 91

flowers, much less have known what kind they were. Accept the fact that you have a spiritual nature—whether you've noticed it or not.

Second, realize your spiritual nature is sinful (Rom. 3:23). Sin is willfully doing something against God or his purposes or just ignoring him—as if he didn't exist or have a plan for your life.

Third, repent or turn away from these sinful attitudes and behavior. God is love and goodness; he will not tolerate evil. So a person who chooses this way of life will eventually come to eternal punishment. But because God loves you and wants you to exist forever with him, he has provided a way for you to change your spiritual nature.

If you have done the first three things, you are ready to accept God's gift of life. This gift is made through Jesus Christ, God's Son. God sent his Son to earth in bodily form to live a perfect life, and then be killed to pay the penalty for the world's—yours and mine—sin. Then he conquered death by rising from the grave. Jesus' death is a "pardon" for you. By accepting this pardon, you can live forever.

The Living Bible, Paraphrased, expresses it this way: "For if you tell others with your own mouth that Jesus Christ is your Lord, and believe in your own heart that God has raised him from the dead, you will be saved. For it is by believing in his heart that a man becomes right with God; and with his mouth he tells others of his faith, confirming his salvation. For the Scriptures tell us that no one who believes in Christ will ever be disappointed" (Rom. 10:9-11).

"To accept Jesus," "to be saved," "to trust in God" all mean the same thing. You accept God's gift of eternal life by accepting what Jesus did for you through his death. You are saved from eternal punishment for those who choose to live in their sinful natures. You trust in God's plan for your life and try to live like he wants you to.

But how can I prove this to you? How can I prove that

God exists, that there is life after death? I can't. No one can. I can only give you evidence. You accept these ideas by faith. Faith means believing in something you haven't seen or which hasn't been proven.

You exercise faith in many areas of life already. You exercise faith that a chair will hold you up before you sit in it. You show faith in manufacturing companies every time you spend money for their products. You show faith in your friends every time you tell them something personal and ask them not to repeat it. People who don't trust or show faith in things and people become paranoid. Faith is necessary to living a normal life.

But the difference in these examples of faith and religious faith is that sometimes you show faith in people or things which let you down. Sometimes you buy a product and later find it defective. Sometimes you show faith in a friend by telling him a personal matter, and that friend uses your secret against you. All people and all things aren't worthy of your faith. God is.

You show faith in the religious realm just as in any other. You accept as truth what God has said through the Bible; you live by it. Truth exists before it is ever proven. Blood circulated through the body long before William Harvey discovered or "proved" it. The continents of the Americans existed long before explorers landed on the shores.

Regardless of proof, truth exists. God exists. Man's soul lives forever.

What does it take to convince someone that there is really life after death? Some have suggested that if there was just proof—if someone could return from the dead—they could believe. Some have returned; many have not yet believed.

Is there life after death? All evidence shouts yes!

Some people are so afraid to die that they never begin to live.
— *Henry Van Dyke*

8
What Dying Says About Living

When one of death's faces turns to you, how will you react? Normally, with grief. Being a Christian does not eliminate sorrow. Jesus wept over his friend Lazarus' death; he grieved over his own death in the hours before his crucifixion. In fact, a Christian may grieve more deeply than a non-Christian because he is more aware of the real meaning of life. We grieve because of earthly separation, not out of a disbelief about life after death. God only commands that the Christian not grieve excessively "as those who have no hope." If your faith is genuine and has been a vital part of your life, it will not fail you in death.

But to sit idly and grieve for missed opportunities is merely for a time. You must move forward; you must decide to go on living.

To move forward does not mean there will never be fear of the future. Fear can be a healthy, creative emotion at times. Fear helps you to accomplish great feats and use time in a meaningful way.

But excessive fear of dying gets in the way of living. You become so obsessed with fear that you can no longer commit yourself to love another person, to work for a cause, to plan for your future. Fear must be tempered with trust in a loving God.

How, then, does one live in the face of death? Be aware of life. Realize that it does not go on forever. Set goals for yourself to accomplish upon earth. In short, as the cliche goes—live each day as if it were your last.

Certainly, you can't wake up each morning and make plans for a rush to the hospital or funeral home. What then does "live each day as if it were your last" mean?

First, it means to make sure you are alive spiritually. Know that your soul will continue to live after death on this earth. If you have doubts about your preparation for that change in existence, go back and read chapter 7. Make sure you are living within God's plan for your life; he has a blueprint especially for you.

Second, to live each day as if it were your last means to strive to grow in mind and character. Exercise your mind by learning about the world around you. Exercise and strengthen your character by rearranging your priorities and values. Invest energy in the present.

Third, to live each day as if it were your last means to reach out to others. Show kindness and love through your attitude, your words, and your actions. Let your family and friends know how much they mean to you.

Fourth, consider the real meaning of life and death. Face the question as to why you are on earth. Discuss questions of life and death and meaningful existence with your family and friends.

To be aware of life means to be aware of life's end—death. This daily, habitual awareness brings comfort and acceptance when you or a loved one is face to face with death.

Only after you've faced death are you ready to live.

Bibliography

Ackerman, Paul R. and Kappleman, Murray M. *Signals: What Your Child Is Really Telling You.* New York: The Dial Press, 1978.

Benton, Richard G. *Death and Dying.* New York: Reinhold Company, 1978.

Bergman, Gwen Smith. "Bearing One Another's Burdens," *Home Life*, March, 1978.

Book, David. "I Love You, Ernie." *event*, March, 1978.

Caughill, Rita W. Ed. *The Dying Patient.* Boston: Little Brown, 1976.

Choron, Jacques. *Suicide.* New York: Scribner, 1972.

Claypool, John. *Tracks of a Fellow Struggler.* Waco, Texas: Word, 1974.

Cornils, Stanley P. *Managing Grief Wisely.* Michigan: Baker Books, 1967.

Easson, Dr. William M. *The Dying Child: The Management of the Child or Adolescent Who Is Dying.* Springfield, Illinois: Charles C Thomas, 1970.

Friess, Horace L. Ed. *Non-Christian Religions A to Z.* New York: Grosset and Dunlap, 1957.

Gatch, Milton Mc C. *Death: Meaning and Morality in Christian Thought and Contemporary Culture.* New York: Seabury Press, 1969.

Glaser, Barney G. and Strauss, Anselm L. *Awareness of Dying.* Chicago: Aldine Publishing Co., 1965.

Gordon, David Cole. *Overcoming the Fear of Death.* New York: Macmillan, 1970.

Grollman, Earl A. Ed. *Concerning Death: A Practical Guide for the Living.* Boston: Beacon Press, 1974.

Grollman, Earl A. Ed. *Explaining Death to Children.* Boston: Beacon Press, 1967.

Grollman, Earl A. *Suicide: Prevention, Intervention, Postvention.* Boston: Beacon Press, 1971.

Hart, Nancy A. and Keidel, Gladys C. "The Suicidal Adolescent." *American Journal of Nursing*, January, 1979.

Jackson, Edgar N. *Understanding Grief.* New York: Abingdon Press, 1957.

Jacobs, Jerry. *Adolescent Suicide.* New York: Wiley-Interscience, John Wiley and Sons, 1971.

Kreis, Bernadine and Pattie, Alice. *Up from Grief.* New York: The Seabury Press, 1969.

Kubler-Ross, Elisabeth. *Death: the Final Stage of Growth.* New Jersey: Prentice-Hall, 1973.

_____. *On Death and Dying.* New York: Macmillan, 1969.

_____. *Questions and Answers on Death and Dying.* New York: Macmillan, 1974.

Kutscher, Austin H. and Kutscher, Lillian G. Eds. *Religion and Bereavement.* New York: Health Sciences Publishing, 1972.

Kutscher, Austin H. and Goldberg, Michael R. Eds. *Caring for the Dying Patient and His Family.* New York: Health Sciences Publishing, 1973.

LeShan, Eda. *Learning to Say Good-By: When a Parent Dies.* New York: Avon, 1976.

Maurer, A. "Adolescent Attitudes Toward Death." *Journal of Genet Psychol* 105: 75-90, September, 1964.

Maxwell, Sister Marie Bernadette. "A Terminally Ill Adolescent and Her Family." *American Journal of Nursing,* May, 1972.

Miller, Randolph Crump. *Live Until You Die.* Philadelphia: United Church Press, 1973.

Mills, Liston O. *Perspectives on Death.* Nashville: Abingdon Press, 1969.

Moody, Raymond, Jr., M.D. *Life After Life.* New York: Bantam Books, 1975.

_____. *Reflections on Life After Life.* New York: Bantam Books, 1977.

Moriarty, David M. M.D. Ed. *The Loss of Loved Ones: The Effects of a Death in the Family on Personality Development.* Springfield, Ill: Charles C Thomas, 1967.

Mormon, Theresa. "When All the Songs Are Sad." *event,* March, 1978.

Neale, Robert E. *The Art of Dying.* New York: Harper and Row, 1973.

Osborne, Ernest. *When You Lose a Loved One.* Public Affairs Pamphlet No. 269, July, 1958.

Osis, Drs. Karlis, and Haraldsson, Erlendur. *At the Hour of Death.* New York: Avon Books, 1977.

Rawlings, Maurice S. *Beyond Death's Door.* New York: Thomas Nelson, 1978.

Reed, Elizabeth L. *Helping Children with the Mystery of Death.* Nashville: Abingdon Press, 1970.

Reeves, Robert B. Ed. *Pastoral Care of the Dying and the Bereaved.* New York: Health Sciences Publishing, 1973.

Schiff, Harriet Sarnoff. *The Bereaved Parent.* New York: Crown, 1977.

Segerberg, Osborn, Jr. *Living with Death.* New York: E. P. Dutton, 1976.

Shepard, Martin, M.D. *Someone You Love Is Dying.* New York: Harmony Books, 1975.

Shneidman, Edwin S. Ed. *On the Nature of Suicide.* San Francisco: Jossey-Bass, 1969.

Vernick, Joel and Lunceford, Janet L. "Milieu Design for Adolescents with Leukemia." *American Journal of Nursing.* 67:559-61, March, 1967.

Verwoerdt, Adriaan, M.D. *Communication with the Fatally Ill.* Springfield, Ill: Charles C Thomas, 1966.

Williams, Dennis A. "Teen-Age Suicide." *Newsweek*, August 28, 1978.

Zim, Herbert S. and Bleeker, Sonia. *Life and Death.* New York: William Morrow, 1970.